AF377770

Cover photo : *Buschsenke* (Skizze), 1985/572-6 (detail).
Courtesy of Galerie Durand Dessert.
Lay-out : Patrick Lébedeff

Special thanks to

Liliane and Michel Durand-Dessert
Jean-Paul Robin
Marc Lefrançois, Gilbert Auréjac (Edimagin)
Tarak Maklouf, Jean-Pierre Riasse
Lydia Wirtz and Frank Wickert

© ÉDITIONS DIS VOIR
3, RUE BEAUTREILLIS
75004 PARIS
ISBN 2-906571-40-7

PRINTED IN FRANCE

GERHARD RICHTER

this series edited by
JACINTO LAGEIRA

in the same series
JEAN-MARC BUSTAMANTE
Christine Macel, Marc Perelman, Jacinto Lageira

DAN GRAHAM
Alain Charre, Marie-Paule Macdonald, Marc Perelman

GERHARD RICHTER

GERTRUD KOCH

LUC LANG

JEAN-PHILIPPE ANTOINE

CONTENTS

The Open Secret
Gerhard Richter and the Surfaces of Modernity

GERTRUD KOCH ▶ 9
translated from the French by BRIAN HOLMES

The Photographer's Hand
Phenomenology in Politics

LUC LANG ▶ 29
translated from the French by ELISABETH HAMILTON

Photography, Painting and the Real
The Question of Landscape in the Painting of Gerhard Richter

JEAN-PHILIPPE ANTOINE ▶ 53
translated from the French by WARREN NIESLUCHOWSKI

Photo Index ▶ 93
Illustrations ▶ 97
About the Artist ▶ 113
Recent Exhibitions ▶ 117
Selected Bibliography ▶ 121

The Open Secret
Gerhard Richter and the Surfaces of Modernity

*F*lowers in a vase, a nude from the back, seascapes, photos, bursting bundles of color alongside monochrome surfaces and black-and-white abstractions alongside skulls and white candles — flipping through catalogue pages in the attempt to recall Gerhard Richter's paintings, one is struck by a double surprise. Not only at the richness and diversity, but even more at the absence of anything surprising. This is precisely what people have always considered characteristic. The individual paintings are a good deal more astounding when one examines them in detail; but that is the difference between an exhibition and a catalogue. Depending on the medium, the work itself changes in perspective. The large canvases of the Alps (or the Himalayas, if you prefer) demolish their photographic origins with something near to pathos; but in their small photographic reproductions they look less like paintings than like photos of photos.

Such trompe-l'oeil effects, produced, as it were, in the margins of the work, spark an awareness of the way the perceptual rules of technics and techniques both merge and violently collide. The major Richter retrospectives of the nineties have underscored this impression by seeking without exception to present his oeuvre in all its facets, leading to the perhaps rash conclusion that it should be conceived as a self-contained whole.

From whatever angle it is approached, Gerhard Richter's work is not easy to identify. It effortlessly runs the gamut of modernity: a glassy sheen of perfection seals it against any hasty grasp, and yet the mirroring surfaces extend a friendly invitation to project our own reflection upon them. This blend of earnestness and irony envelops the viewer in its shifting play, which is based on a combination of epistemological and aesthetic perspectives. As a commentary on the mutual infiltration of visual, photographic, and painterly possibilities, but also as a reaction to them, Richter's work raises an echo in the soundproof space where its disparate elements refer to one another.

Within all this diversity one central and symptomatic motif can be observed, which might be described as the vertigo of perspectives. Not only does it determine the spatial structure of the abstract paintings, but its abrogation of focus and depth effects a troubling break with the epistemic magic of illusionism. The philosophical upheavals of modernity and the dissolution of the certainties borne by traditional world views have bought about more than one Copernican revolution in our relation to the universe, creating a specific longing for reality and for a corresponding representation of it. Thus it may be said that with the illusionistic gains of Renaissance perspective, with the possibility of three-dimensional representation, there arises the suspicion that modernity's discourse of appearances actually coincides with doubt — not a doubt about the existence of the real, but rather about its comprehensibility beyond the limited problems of representation. What comes to the fore is the world's opacity, a veil rendering it impenetrable to consciousness. At the same time, with this philosophical figure of a divided world composed of things and alien consciousnesses all indifferent to the observer, the plurality of experiential worlds fades into a model of infinitely simultaneous surfaces which can only be touched tangentially. It will henceforth be possible to clip endlessly multiple perspectives from this single world, without ever being able to recompose them, even virtually, into a "total picture."

Richter constantly refers us back to such epistemological problems, both in his own descriptions of his works and in the objectifications they present to us. In many respects these references can be read as commentaries on the oldest problem of pictorial reproduction, that of figural representation: how can three-dimensional objects be reproduced on two-dimensional surfaces, or in short, how can spatial dimensions best be shown flat? Only against this background can one clearly perceive an obsession of Richter's oeuvre that develops in two directions, one formalist and the other expressive. The formalist direction is the path of art history, the roadmap of possibilities and constructions. The expressive direction is the path itself in isolation, the journey through the spatiality of surface, its reinvention.

Objectivity

And what if, at bottom, there were nothing at all?
And what if, at bottom, there were nothingness?
And what if it had nothing to do with Uncle Rudi?
And what if Uncle Rudi were only an image?

And what if the painting "Uncle Rudi" were not an image of Uncle Rudi?
Is the image "Uncle Rudi" then an image of Nothingness?
Who says that the photo of Uncle Rudi is an image of Uncle Rudi,
And who says that Richter's painting is a photo of Uncle Rudi,
And who says that the photo of Uncle Rudi was nothing,
That only Richter's painting is an image of Uncle Rudi,
Of his petty nullity, a laughing man in a uniform,
An image which shows "everything"?
Everything lies, everything illusion, nothing to see, everything to know?

Kurt Drawert has written a tale with a photo at its center, a photo which a grandson finds in one of his grandfather's chests in the attic. On this photo is his grandfather in a Wehrmacht uniform, and on the back is written: "For the Führer, the Folk and the Fatherland — Christmas 1941."[1] The photo contradicts the grandfather's biography, as recounted by himself to the grandson. This fictive photo from literature provides the departure point for another writer's philosophical developments on the status of photography:

Here the word "photo" stands for a complex of implicit theories and practices of the reproduction of reality. Most people use certain standardized means to orient themselves in their relations with one another and with the world. Some of these means are held to be relatively untrustworthy, others to be highly accurate. In the twentieth century, photos are widely recognized as particularly sure reproductions. The field of the imagination is covered by literature, painting, and the performing arts; that of factuality, by photography.[2]

When a photo becomes the object of a painting, imagination is not simply put *in the place* of factuality; rather, a discourse on

---

[1] Kurt Drawert, *Spiegelland, Ein Deutscher Monolog* (Frankfurt, 1992), p. 59.
[2] Herbert Hrachovec, "Photogene Enttäuschungen," in *Deutsche Zeitschrift für Philosophie* # 4, 1995 (in preparation).

imagination and factuality begins, along with a discourse on the hegemony of particular media of representation.

It is well known that the invention of photography and later of film dealt some powerful blows to painting. And this for two reasons, whose relation is paradoxical. When photography first appeared in the classical domains of portrait and landscape painting it was perceived as a shocking and threatening *creatio ex nihilo*; and yet it had the same origins as the type of figurative painting which it was assumed to rival. Like an illegitimate off-spring of the nobler arts, photography reproduced once again the equivocal breakthroughs provoked by the "discovery" or "in-vention" of perspective in the Renaissance. Like the latter, photo-graphy too would lend itself to questions and purposes both scientific and artistic. The arts and techniques of spatial repre-sentation, which culminated in the specific illusionist aesthetic still linked to the concept of the Renaissance, trace their origins back through the *camera obscura* to the same sources from which photography would spring. Thus it is no exaggeration to maintain a cultural-historical theory like that of Erwin Panofsky, who interprets perspective as a "symbolic form."[3]

From this perspective on perspective, the war between figura-tive painting and photography looks less like a struggle between the old and the new, and much more like the soap opera of illegi-timate offspring who finally seek to reclaim their family inheri-tance, with well-founded proof to boot. What is genuinely new in the photographic development of the *camera obscura* is not so much photography's capacity to produce the trompe-l'oeil effects of illusionism as its way of rendering the subject anonymous — the subject which central perspective registered as an identical

---

[3] Erwin Panofsky, "Die Perspective als 'symbolische Form,'" in *Vorträge der Bibliothek Warburg* (1924-1925), vol. IV; English translation, *Perspective as a symbolic form* (New York: Zone Books, 1991), tr. Christopher S. Wood.

positioning of the creator's and beholder's standpoint, during the glorious early days of the rise of the bourgeoisie.

The "vertigo of knowledge" that Hegel invokes in *The Phenomenology of Mind* — and that we rediscover in the obsessive blurring whereby Richter destroys the surface of the photo — remains bound to the experience of modern subjectivity, which is no longer confronted by a preestablished order but caught up in a floating state of vertigo out of which its must always recover its stance, get back on its feet. This toppling over from the epistemological certainty of central perspective to doubts abouts "illusion" (by way of reproductibility and "true-to-life" rendition) takes place initially in Baroque painting:

> The diagonal as the principal orientation of Baroque painting is already a blow to the tectonics of the image, negating or at least obscuring the orthogonality of the scenic structure (Heinrich Wölfflin, 1915). The figure loses its firm position, the "tectonic basis" fades into secondary status.

> [...Already] G. B. Tiepolo "lets illusion veer into uncertainty" (Werner Busch). Illusion is no longer a puzzling riddle; artistic means have become autonomous, in a premonition of full artistic autonomy.[4]

The destabilization carried out by Tiepolo is the first tug at a state of equilibrium that will finally be upset by photography, which prolongs a movement that Jeannot Simmens has described as a "paradoxical *ecstasy of precision*."[5] The complement of art's autonomization involves the resolution of the "puzzling riddle" in a quite different direction, that of science. The illusionistic painting of the puzzle-picture, which on a single surface regroups two objects that can only be distinguished from the spectator's

---

[4] Jeannot Simmen, *Vertigo: Schwindel der modernen Kunst* (Munich: Klinckhardt und Biermann/ Zeit Zeuge Kunst), p. 14 *sq*.
[5] *Ibid.*

viewpoint, puts the riddle of the "deceptive similarity" between image and nature at our mental disposition. Where art in its purely imitative relation could formerly be interpreted as "aping nature," now it makes itself fully independent. Thus it hands over the apprehension and representation of nature to philosophy and the theory of knowledge on the one hand, and to the empirical natural sciences on the other.

Photography brings these two sundered paths of development back together. The apparatus elaborated on the basis of the *camera obscura* will be considered simultaneously as an observational instrument (Muybridge) — the "pencil of nature" (Talbot) — and as an expressive aesthetic medium. This raises a new set of problems. Where illusionist perspective produced an identity between subject and object (insofar as the perspective of the former on the latter made the object the creation of the subject and indeed part of it), the photographic apparatus no longer asserts anything about the identity of subject and object, but only about the identity of the object and its image. The photograph will be understood as a material trace of the object, light radiation captured by chemical means. Photography creates this identity between the object and its image without the recourse to or concourse of a subject, since even the release of the shutter can be automated.

It is against this background that Richter sets not only his *Uncle Rudi* [ill. 2] but also a great many other portraits. By defining every increase in resemblance as an illusion that must be overcome through sublation [*Aufhebung*], he adds another twist to the spiral arising from the endless overcoming and negation of the "objective," or the transformation of the figure into abstraction. If one wished to seize only a *single* movement running throughout Richter's work, perhaps it would be this spiral without beginning or end, which can be prolonged without ever repeating or reaching the limit of its resources, and which nonetheless represents an element of coherence — or produces this coherence as a principle of representation.

The painting *Uncle Rudi* does not deny the proximity of photography, nor contest its capacity to produce resemblance; its simply asks a new question about identity. Upon the picture of a pipe painted according to the rules of illusionism, Magritte had written that this was *not* a pipe. The cognitive refinement of this joke on the difference between signifier and signified is overrated; but Richter's painted commentary on photography gives the problem a heightened charge, which draws it back to the center of objectivity itself.

A laughing man in the uniform of a Wehrmacht soldier on leave, coiffed in a visor cap with eagle, sporting epaulettes that give him a vague rank of officer: the painting with the title *Uncle Rudi* dissolves the photograph. The swastika clasped in the eagle's claws on the cap can only be projected by association; the military rank slips away in the wavering contours. *Uncle Rudi* is no longer a scandalous exception in the family history. It lacks the meticulous accuracy that sets detective Drawert, in his photography story, on the hereditary track of a petty-bourgeois family's political bad faith. Richter's *Uncle Rudi* is incomparably more abstract than the literary figure evoked by Drawert. And this abstraction from the indexical gesture of the photograph is precisely what induces the process of generalization that makes the painting such a resonant body.

Like Richter's other photo-paintings, *Uncle Rudi* is an agonistic confrontation with an objectivity that has seemingly been lost to photography. Unlike the photo-realists, Richter does not seek to mimetically or ironically outdo the advantages of photography, but rather to skirt around them through mimicry. The exactitude of the photographs brings out an inexactitude that appears above all to be caused by the social practice of photography as a popular mass medium.

The landscape postcard, the family snapshot, the quickly taken passport photo or portrait: all are hectic emanations of fleeting events that long ago lost their character as events, simply because they now take place every day. The sad splendor of these images is not due, as Walter Benjamin thought, to the overload of multiple reproduction and simultaneous presence, but to the lost aura of the subject, who can no longer see him- or herself as a part of mass ornamentation:

> There is no shared thinking between the ornament and the masses who manufacture it. As linear as it may be, no line stretches from the mass particles to the total figure. It resembles aerial views of landscapes and cities, in that it does not grow from within a given reality but appears above them.... The more its composition is reduc-ed pure linearity, the more its immanence withdraws from the consciousness of those who give it form.[6]

> As low as the value of the mass ornament may sink, its degree of reality remains higher than that of artistic productions, still attempting the recondite culture of higher sentiments in outworn forms; but these no longer mean anything at all.[7]

These early observations by Siegfried Kracauer descibe quite precisely the continuing process of constant twisting and toppling whereby the aesthetic problems of representation converge around

---

[6] Siegfried Kracauer, "Das Ornament der Masse" (1928), in *Schriften* (Frankfurt-am-Main: Suhrkamp, 1990), vol. 5, 2, p. 57.
[7] *Ibid.*, p. 60.

the decentering of the subject, whether in the modern masses, in the romantic splitting of the self, or in the different social practices of photography and photo-painting.

The specific aesthetic rationality of the mass ornament does not only unfold on the level of adequation, but also in a specific relation to nature. To the extent that it enourages the desubstantialization of nature, it contributes to a rationalized relation to the natural world. The ornament does not conceive the body as a falsely organic whole, but rather makes its "segments" into the component parts of a "composition" that stresses the body's abstraction and artificiality. Thus the symbolic or semiotic character of the ornament becomes its specific quality:

> Only the scraps of human totality enter the mass ornament. Their selection and integration in the aesthetic medium stems more directly from the principle of form-shattering reason than from any attempt to preserve the organic unity of man.[8]

The "aerial views" of cities, bodies, and landscapes that Kracauer discovered in modern mass ornaments make their appearance again in Richter's photo-paintings; and thereby we more clearly understand why his method is one of mimicry, or better, why he can grasp the ornament itself as mimicry.

"Aerial views" are known for two predominant qualities: they are taken from a great distance (like snapshots from a bird's-eye perspective, if one seeks to fit them into the familiar genres of photography); and they are "blurred," as though the camera had malfunctioned, giving them a feeling of movement that runs counter to our expectations of correct photographic reproduction. Richter's paintings draw their tension from these two characteristics, which are emphasized by the fact that he takes away the color and at the

---

[8] *Ibid.*, p. 64.

same time undercuts the graphic qualities of black-and-white photography by his impasto application of pigment.

The formal advantages of this technique can be read directly from a painting like *Uncle Rudi*. The effects of desubjectification and stereotyping that photography inevitably brings are represented by Richter through the aesthetic practice of abstraction and minimalization, thus baring the open secret of the camera, which is that the fulfilment of its implicit promise, the promise that "everyone can be filmed" — once upheld as a guaranteed right by Walter Benjamin — comes at the very moment when the emphatic reference to the subject has melted away. The names are glued uselessly beneath the photos, because the photos themselves are no longer taken seriously as the names of people and things, as they were, for example, in the early days of portrait photography. The newspaper clippings and family photos that underly Richter's paintings or are laid to rest in his monumental *Atlas* — like a *Dictionary of Received Ideas* in the spirit of Flaubert — take on their seriousness in quite another way, as memories of the dead.

Let us return again to *Uncle Rudi*. This painting of 1965 refers us to a parallel date. The major study *Un art moyen: Essai sur les usages sociaux de la photographie* also appeared in 1965. The authors, including Pierre Bourdieu and Luc Boltanski (the brother of Christian[9]), studied cerain aspects of photography as a function of social categories, for example, "barbaric taste."[10] These individual studies all lead to the impression that photography as a mass phenomenon has left its specific mark on a visual epoch which is incapable of deciphering itself:

> It seems as though photography were the expression of an implicit aesthetic, which rests content with the most economical of means

---

[9] Monika Steinhauser pointed out to me that Luc Boltanski is Christian Boltanski's brother.
[10] P. Bourdieu, L. Boltanski, R. Castel, J-C. Chamboredon, *Un art moyen: Essai sur les usages sociaux de la photographie* (Paris: Minuit, 1965), p. 113.

and objectifies itself in a certain type of images, without ever being able (by its very essence) to recognize itself for what it is.[11]

The early photographers had at least in part attempted to ennoble their photography by impressionistically dissolving its aesthetic naturalism in a softening of contours, as though to deny the "implicit aesthetic" of the medium. Richter takes the opposite path: in his painting he points to the implicit aesthetic of photography as a social phenomenon.

This is what renders *Uncle Rudi* so ghostlike: all that remains of him in the blurry gray image is what characterizes him as a type. The laughing man in the on-leave uniform of the Wehrmacht, the supposed officer with the probable swastika on his cap, is so uncanny because on one hand, he *is* the "uncle Rudi"[12] who is apparently represented here on the photo and whom we must assume to be a real individual; while on the other, he has been deconstructed as an individual in order to reveal his type. What stays with us is the impression of a man pleased with himself, standing with his legs slightly apart in front of a wall for the sole reason that a photo of him is about to be taken:

> The photo captures this memory. In most cases one would be unable to remember why and about what one was laughing. The photo testifies at least that one has laughed heartily.[13]

All the horror that Richter's painting communicates to us springs from the spectral tracing of this *hearty* laugh, which arises in memory as something typical, near, familiar. One might also say that with this painterly metamorphosis of the photo Richter has found a visual equivalent of what Hannah Arendt, in her

[11] *Ibid.*, p. 116.

[12] Perhaps it is worth recalling that *Uncle Rudi* was painted from one of Richter's own family photos. It is indeed a photo of Richter's uncle Rudi. See Benjamin Buchloh, "Geteiltes Gedächtnis: Zwei Skulpturen für einen Raum von Palermo," in the catalogue of the 1994 *Gerhardt Richter* retrospective (Stuttgart: Cantz, 1994), vol. II, *Texte*, p. 30.

[13] Bourdieu, *op. cit.*, p. 39.

famous title, referred to as "the banality of evil."[14]

In *Uncle Rudi*, however, Richter has not only captured an historical motif that emerges through memory into the perception of the present. After all, he adopts the same approach to other subjects: a number of the *Eight Student Nurses* (1966) also laughed heartily when they were photographed, just as Boltanski's dead Swiss sometimes did. The relations one can establish are therefore not only directly linked to the history of a particular subject, but also to the wider history of representation. In this way, Richter can use his paradoxical figures to inscribe himself in the drama of representation, which he restages without any parody. Richter quite rightly refuses to admit that he is merely quoting or repertorying the rhetorical figures of painting. He once designated his photo-paintings as "dubious gifts" [*Kuckuckseier*, literally "cuckoo's eggs"] which people take for something other than what they really are.[15]

Blind Spots in the Mirror

The notion of an unclouded Mirror of Nature is the notion of a mirror which would be indistinguishable from what was mirrored, and thus would not be a mirror at all. The notion of a human being whose mind is such an unclouded mirror, and who knows this, is the image... of God.[16]

The reprise of the mirror metaphor for the drama of representation in photography brings up a number of interesting problems, which may be described as forming a part of the spiral that coils through the enormous radius of Richter's oeuvre. His work contains various versions of a negative commentary on the "spotless mirror," the phantasm of a three-thousand-year-old quarrel

[14] Hannah Arendt, *Eichmann in Jerusalem: A Report on the Banality of Evil* (London: Faber and Faber, 1963).
[15] Interview between Gerhard Richter and Benjamin Buchloh, in *Gerhardt Richter*, *op. cit.*, vol. II, p. 94.
[16] Richard Rorty, *Philosophy and the Mirror of Nature* (Oxford: Basil Blackwell, 1980), p. 376.

over the interdiction of images which finally states only this: because creation is in the very image of God there must be no other images resembling the objects they represent. The empty mirror can only be the sign of an absence, which is why it refers to the existence of objects. Now, Richter is not the only one to understand the mirror as the aesthetic sign of the void. Glass and mirrors in their use as aesthetic materials seem, like the camera, to undercut the problem of objectivity versus abstraction. But far more than the camera which, even when automated, still produces images fixed in space and time, glass and mirrors can offer a mobility entirely devoted to and dependent upon the movement of the viewer. Transparent glass with its possibilities for perspectival refraction and the mirror as a generator of images constitute two imaginary poles that allow for the overcoming or sublation of two distinct traditions: that of imitation-resemblance (mirror) and that of formal abstraction, or the very process of seeing itself (glass).

Both of these can be understood as reflections on the end of perspectival representation and on its continuity in perception which, in Richter's work, leads not accidentally to monochrome painting. In an exemplary study, Bernhard Lypp has demonstrated the complete turnabout from irony to mysticism in the lineage from Duchamp to Ad Reinhardt. In an essay on "mirror paintings" he has analyzed Duchamp's work *Tu m'* (1918, oils and pencil on canvas, with bottle brush, three safety pins, and a nut):

> The canvas is presented metaphorically as a blank sheet of paper, and our gaze is invited to pass through it, insofar as we see that a group of colors and forms on one side corresponds to a group of colors and forms on the other...

The blank sheet must thus be understood as something like an open window, *una finestra aperta*, through which our gaze passes in search of its transformation. Duchamp ironizes this mysterious transformation which is thought to be carried out on the canvas.[17]

Duchamp's strategy of irony consists in interpreting the entire system of representation as an ensemble of interlocking semiotic conventions, thus referring to the idea that the world and life itself must be conceived as a system of signs: "We can therefore replace the *fenestra aperta* with a glass allowing us to see the world as a single artificial still life, in which the essence of our own images and those of others will be included."[18] Richter refers to this pole of modern art's development in one aspect of his work (*Four Glass Panels*, 1967 [ill. 3]), while dealing with another pole with his series *Gray* (1970 [ill. 7]). Prominent here is the monochromy that Lypp sees as paradigmatic in the work of Ad Reinhardt:

> It [Reinhardt's art] is the example of an artistic gesture occupying the symbolic space to which we have been brought by the self-reflexivity of painting, understanding the monochrome painting as the exemplification of a fundamentally artistic world view... What occurs on the monochrome or simply monotone canvas is the systematic disappearance of the visible world in its everyday form. The spectator of this disappearance is then begged to embark on his own disappearance, abandoning his distance from the art object and replacing it with an expressely religious devotion.[19]

Between Duchamp's attempt at an irony which collapses the diverse spheres of the real into a single world of art and Reinhardt's quest to dissolve the entire world into a colored surface, Richter's work can be readily interpreted as an inclusive strategy employing all the available directions as rhetorical figures, thus providing a post-modern response to the feverish seriousness of both the ironists and the mystics of modernity (to use Lypp's expressions).

---

[17] Berhard Lypp, "Spiegel-Bilder," in *Was ist ein Bild?* (Munich: Fink, 1994), ed. Gottfried Boehm, p. 430.

[18] *Ibid.*, p. 431.

[19] *Ibid.*, p. 432 *sq.* Lypp pursues his argument to show the turn toward the theological-mystical figures that characterize this path of modernity, notably in Reinhardt's space and shadow installations, which I will not discuss here.

And it seems that the case must rest there, since no more decisive formulation is in the offing.

To me, however, this assessment of Richter's work seems not entirely accurate. Richter's experiments with colored mirrors (whose gray or blood-red tinted glass tends more to swallow up than to reflect the veiled or masked image of the world) still share certain aspects with the so-called photo-paintings, of which *Uncle Rudi* is far from being the last example; and the gray mirrors themselves continue appearing on into the nineties, in parallel with the monochromes and the abstract paintings. I do not interpret this simultaneity as a purely ironic self-overcoming, but quite to the contrary, as a reciprocal confirmation of the reference to a common problem, that is, the blurring of the object. Whether in *Uncle Rudi* or in the *October 18, 1977* cycle (1988 [ill. 21]) on the death of the terrorists in Stammheim, or again in the motif of the self's oblivion in an opaque or colored mirror, what characterizes these paintings is the reference to the temporality of our imagination, the haziness of our memory, its vagueness, the sinking into amnesia, the disappearance and blurring.[20] As viewers of these paintings we are reminded of our own past; we see ourselves disappear, in the truest sense of the phrase, before our very eyes; in broken outlines we recognize forms that appear familiar and yet withdraw into the distance. Just a step farther and we would see ourselves with a death's head (*Skull*, 1983 [ill.15]) and white candles strangely flickering (*Two Candles*, 1982 [ill. 14]). And of course Richter knows full well that it does not really work that way, that scattered fragments of narrative can no longer make up a happy story, even if it were the ironic history of the rhetoric of fine art:

---

[20] See Gertrud Koch, "The Richter-Scale of Blur," in *October* #62, 1992.

The only paradox is that I always begin with the intention of obtaining a closed picture, with a properly composed motif. Then, with a relatively great effort, I proceed to destroy this intention piece by piece, against my own will almost, until the picture is finished — that is, until it has nothing left besides openness.[21]

Richter's work maintains a rather more complex specular relation with the modern tradition than it might seem at first sight. His doubt does not only lead to the ironic gesture of outdoing the rhetorical formulae through overemphasis, but also to the veiled tragedy that broodingly and agonistically opposes such gestures.[22]

Richter's Annunciation after Titian

The collapse of metaphysics rips through the veils, yet without revealing anything behind them — just as in the azure vaults of Baroque *trompe-l'œil* ceilings, the heavens open to display only the fleshy foot of a rather rustic angel-boy. What Richter has recovered from the collapse of metaphysics is abstract movement. This he casts over the surface. Looking at the *Annunciation after Titian* (three paintings, 1973 [ill. 11]), it again becomes clear that what occurs here is not simply an analogy between the pictorial techniques of the Old Masters and the abstraction of the Moderns.

[21] Interview with Gerhard Richter by Benjamin Buchloh in *Gerhard Richter: Paintings* (London: Thames and Hudson, 1988), ed. Roald Nagaard, p. 27. In the previously quoted interview with Buchloh, Richter declares: "I see no sense in demonstrating the lost possibilities of painting. For me it's a matter of saying something, of new possibilities.... The whole and every detail provokes a feeling, releases an atmosphere (*Stimmung*)" (in *Gerhardt Richter*, op. cit., vol. II, p. 95). Richter is of course familiar with the ambiguity encountered by all artists who can no longer make use of the avant-garde as an *aesthetic practice* (and not only as a historical movement representing a now exhausted aesthetic practice). What seems to separate Richter from postmodernism is simply that he does not consider it a solution to the problem of the exhaustion of the modern.

[22] See Brigit Pelzer, "Das tragische Begehren," in *Gerhardt Richter* catalogue, op. cit., vol. II. Her esaay on Richter attempts to link the tragic structure of desire in Lacan to a kind of psycho-history of the pictorial imagination. However, her analysis stays rather closer to the movement of desire than to the paintings.

Rather, there is a complex inscription in a canon of problems which has become, so to speak, the visual signature of monotheism. Revelation must immediately be veiled in its representation; the numinosity of the divine cannot be objectified, but can only shine forth in appearance. We find the metaphysics of light in Christian painting in the form of representations of the heavens, of the Annunciation, or in Richter's *Annunciation after Titian*. We find it in the work of Barnett Newman, Mark Rothko, or Ad Reinhardt, but there again as veiling in monochromy or as a luminous trace appearing on the borders of the monochrome surface.[23]

For Richter, the radicality of the monochrome is a kind of magnifying mirror, just as one can see Roy Lichtenstein as a master of enlargement who uses it to rediscover, like no one else, the lost face of detail. Richter's abstract paintings have a kind of thickening that refers above all to a deep space which has become completely impossible to paint, since perspective has learned to turn entirely around its own axis. For the amazing thing in Richter's abstract paintings is not only their technical perfection, but the dynamic organization of space that makes them seem almost three-dimensional, arousing an abstract illusion of spatial depth, layer upon layer, to the point where one is almost stirred to look behind the canvas.

Were this the case, Richter would have come all the way back to Duchamp's move through perspective into real space. Nonetheless, I see what is "new" in Richter's *Annunciation* as a further turn of the spiral. The interpenetration of art, the world, and life is no longer an aesthetic program, but topples backward, or for-

---

[23] See. Georg Syamken, "Mark Rothko und Barnett Newman: Ihr Verhältnis zu 2. Moses 20/4," in *Babylon: Beiträge für jüdischen Gegenwart* # 12, 1993. Syamken underlines the relations these two artists maintained with Man Ray and Marcel Duchamp, relations founded on the biographies of groups of painters; thus one again sees the clear symmetry between the ready-made, surrealism, and photography on one hand, and the abstractionists, minimalists, and conceptualists on the other. These are two poles of one continuous linear movement.

ward, as you will, into illusion, into the unconditionality of transcendence: a luminance shining on — or from — something other.[24]

---

[24] On the impossibility of overcoming transcendence in the realm of the aesthetic, see Gottfried Boehm, "Die Bilderfrage," in *Was ist ein Bild?*, *op. cit.*, p. 340, where Boehm refers to the painting of Rothko: "The color is organized in a series of semi-transparent layers. It is articulated in a logic of disappearance which forms part of painting's primal reality. The first trace of painting applied by the painter of the most ancient past, the very first layer of representation negates the ground of the painting and brings it forth anew in the same moment.... Negation is at the basis of all pictorial appearance."

The Photographer's Hand[*]
Phenomenology in Politics

Shots

*K*nowing that these are most often oils on canvas in no way dissipates the uneasiness you may feel in front of a painting by Gerhard Richter, so problematical is it to identify these images. They really are paintings and yet you feel as though you were looking at photographs or, more exactly, paintings of a photographic nature.

If you begin to scrutinize the landscapes that are part of his work — and one of the most consecrated motifs in the tradition of painting — you will find that they are most often neutral, insignificant and anonymous, as though they had frozen the instant eyes fell on them and that despite the titles indicating specific sites, they could indifferently and haphazardly evoke almost any region in a temperate climate. His skies, gray or blue, spreading and hazy, that often occupy a good half of the canvass (*Wiesental*, 1985/572 4; *Chinon*, 1987/644.645) are devoid of any of the qualities or singular beauty that might be conferred on them by color, luminosity or a group of clouds with its curves, billows, nebulosities and, say, its

*Nota Bene: A)- This is a remodeled and expanded version of a text originally published as *La main du photographe,* in an exhibition catalogue, *Peinture, Emblèmes et Références,* CAPC de Bordeaux, December 1993. B)- The numbers following the dates given for Richter's paintings are references to the *Catalogue raisonné,* Kunst und Ausstellunqshalle der Bundesrepublik Deutschland, 1993.

moving fissures.[1] Indeed, landscape painting is never simply referential; if and when it does in fact depict a particular place, it is consistently an attempt to attain the essence of the landscape: symbolic, psychological, geographical or other.

With respect to this tradition, Richter's landscapes express a great poverty in point of view, or even an absence of vision, but rather than invoking weak or faulty composition, it would be more appropriate to speak of platitude in framing, as if these images were not some Sunday painter's but more what you might expect from an amateur photographer for whom these shots had no other value than vacation souvenirs. This would be justifying the photographic nature of Richter's landscapes on such formal or aesthetic criteria alone, were there not an additional and decisive element in the perception of these paintings. Indeed, all the contours are "tremblé"[5] and out-of focus. This is true for objects in both mid and background. If these really were photographs, we might conclude that the blurriness is due to the shots being too poor to have ever been so enlarged or that they were taken with the focus on some object in the foreground that has since been cropped. This blurriness associated with enlargement or miscalculated depth of field is a notion strictly optical and photographic, no criteria for the practice of painting.[2] As for the portraits and genre scenes, the prosaic quality of the motifs, the banality of the framing and the seeming instantaneity in the capture of images added to the fact that the images are most often rendered in black and white oils,[3] would make for nothing more than an endless evocation of vacation and family snapshots, news reels, fashion and

[1] Richter's skies are not expressionist or lyrical as in Italian baroque paintings or today's postcards except when they appear in isolation, decontextualized or simply above the ocean with which their relation is not simply mimetic or mirroring. Richter sets up strange photographic disjunction s in depth of field between sea and sky.

[2] The desire to blur the contours of things represented in painting has been around for quite a while, witness Leonardo Da Vinci's *sfumato* and the Impressionist's *touches*. But in both of these cases what was at stake was to show the effects of light dispersion due to natural causes: mist, fog, smoke, whereas here it is a phenomenon linked to problems in photographic technique.

[3] A black and white oil *facture* that is not part of the figurative tradition which only used these "colors" in drawing, pastels, watercolors and engraving, for reasons having nothing to do with Richter's.

pornographic magazines, etc., if it were not for the fact that much of the perceptual data makes the reference to photography decisive. The blurriness we observe in the landscapes is here compounded by the effects of "filé"[4], "bougé"[5] *(Sekretärin, 1964/14; Reisebüro, 1966/120)* as well as under- and over-exposure *(Frau mit Kind (Strand) 1965/73; Motorboot (I. Fassung) 1965/79 79 a)*. All of these are notions of perception and ways of reading images that I could not even evoke nor Richter paint if photography did not exist.[6] The first work in the *Catalogue raisonné* (1962-1993)[7] entitled *Tisch* that the artist himself has called the originary painting — the one which began his research — looks like a black and white painting of a press photograph. As if it were a question of admitting, before even thinking about the practice of painting, that in this second half of the 20th century we live in a world of images,[8] where producing the visible is more likely to involve photographic techniques, which also have the advantage of being simpler, more immediate and closer to ocular perception.[9]

[4] le filé: When the mouvement of the subject of the shot is visible in a still, because the shooter is left open, long enough to capture it.

[5] le tremblé; le bougé: When a photographic image looks blurred or "shaky" because the camera or its operator moves or trembles while the shot is being taken.

[6] Also true for the *Gilbert & George* (1975/380.381 1.2) paintings where Richter proceeds by superimposition or what would appear to be multiple exposure.

[7] Published by Kunst und Ausstellungshalle der Bundesrepublik Deutschland, 1993.

[8] Today, even people that are interested in painting discover it principally through catalogues and magazines. As for art school students, they learn the history of painting through photography. When people actually go to see a painting in its physical reality, the original is apprehended, in the worst of cases, as a more or less good copy of its own reproduction, and in the best, as a relic that validates the photograph. But we have known all this since Malraux and his "imaginary museum" and Thierry de Duve's work on Duchamp, particularly: *Résonnances du ready-made,* Jacqueline Chambon, 1989.

[9] "... the analog photographic image (...) can be characterized by (...) the resemblance of the image of an object to the way human eyes perceive it." (...) "But," adds Jean-Marie Schaeffer: "Asupplementary constraint in the analogy is the fact that the phototonic image requires a specific modalization that ranges from the choice of certain lenses and the inversion of the negative into a positive, to the prevalence of the snapshot." In *L'image précaire*, Seuil, coll. Poétique, 1987, p. 17-18.

In his work, Richter's apprehension of this reality is radical. As if photography were, *for us,* the origin of all images and had begun to exist before a form of painting that could only explore its own tekhné with criteria inherited from photography. The practice of painting would, from the outset, involve conceiving and composing images with notions of framing, montage, speed, depth of field, quantity of light, medium gray, emulsion quality, etc.... Such that when Richter paints, if you will, like a photographer converted to painting, he readily expresses the discovery of two distinct distances:

The first distance: from the eye to the hand, the distance to which painters are accustomed, paint and brushwork are as sharp as direct imprints on the canvas.

The second distance: from the viewfinder to the subject, the photographer's distance, in which spots of light have in the best instance the sharpness of an indirect print on the film, that which is obtained through a phototonic flux. This discovery by no means leads us to compare the sharpness of each image but to understand that there are effectively two different kinds of images, one which is the result of a mechanical impression and another which is the result of of a physiochemical impression, in which visibility manifests itself very differently. So it is that when Richter "paints photographs" of lighted candles *(Zwei Kerzen, 1982/499 1. 2* [ill. 14]; *Kerze, 1983/546 2),* or even of certain landscapes *(Landschaft bei Koblenz, 1987/640)* you must step back farther from the canvas than the hand-to-eye distance in order to see the images appear "in focus." Yet when you approach the canvas, the "photographic" image blurs and the paint is smooth and absent, almost immaterial, like a print on paper.

However, when Richter "paints paintings" of woodlands, for example *(Parkstück, 1971/310.311)*, with a painterly and gestural *facture*, stepping back avails you a vision of a park bathed in warm and contrasting light and stepping up to the canvas you see beyond the blur of representation to a second sharpness, that of the pictoral material applied to canvas. As if photography were an assertion of intervals and distances that can not be crossed[10] and painting, always sharp, a statement in the back-and-forth from farthest to nearest. Photography is thus in the order of an image's optical definition whereas painting is indifferently optical or haptic.[11] This is why, when working on a canvas that is at once a photograph and a painting, Richter sometimes places the "photographed faces" in the mid-ground, and the brushwork not in the foreground, but better, on the very surface of the canvas, such that two images of a very different nature appear. These are images which can not be compared, as the first belongs to the virtual depth of representation and the second, to a real surface of presentation *(Herr Baker / Frau Baker / Mädchen Baker / Junge Baker, 1965)*. If the photographed portraits of the Bakers nonetheless appear blurred, it must be that that by putting the emphasis on the perceptive reality of a painter at work,[12] he focuses on the canvas, converting the distance from the eye to the painting-

[10] Even when this is no farther than the depth of focus, the focal distance from the lens to the film. "Because photography is a print of something at a distance, it is from the beginning situated in a spatial tension that implies the absence of any direct contact between imprinter and print. In other words, before it has anything to do with mirroring, it is first a question of distance: it is the result of spatial distension." Jean-Marie Schaeffer, op.cit., note 9, p.17.

[11] I borrow this useful concept from Deleuze who borrowed it from Riegl in the first edition of his *Spätromische Kunstindustrie* (1901) and that he defines as follows: "We can use the word *haptic* any time t.3 vision itself discovers its own sense of touch, a sense that belongs only to it, and that is distinct from the eye's optical function. You might say in this case that the painter paints with his eyes, but only to the extent that he can touch with his eyes. And without a doubt, this haptic function can have its plenitude directly and all at once, in antique forms for which we have (Egyptian art). But it can also be recreated in the 'modern' eye starting with manual violence and insubordination." In *Logique de la Sensation, Francis Bacon*, la Difference, 1984, p.89.

[12] With much perversity, certainly, and so much the better.

hand into a focal distance; the concrete surface of the canvas thus becomes a sharp foreground that relegates the photographic figures emerging in the fiction of the mid and backgrounds[13] to blurriness. This discovery, which concerns the nature and not the degree of these two heterogeneous worlds of image that Richter unceasingly works at confronting in the very experience of painting, defuses and voids the debate about figuration and non-figuration in painting.

If in a culture which is no longer religious but secular, the objects that have lost all sacredness and the beings that have lost all divinity are more readily and pertinently grasped through photography, so be it! Richter duly sets this down[14] and, with few exceptions, all of his figurative paintings belong to the world of photographic images.[15] If representation can no longer appear in painting without a reference to photography, then Richter will paint a photographed world. All of which puts his landscapes, portraits and genre scenes beyond any suspicion of academicism, despite the fact that in this case the photographs are paintings.

[13] It is interesting to note that in Betty (1988/*663 5*), the young woman's arm and left shoulder in the photographic foreground are, in the painting, almost sharp (but not however, and for a very good reason, flush with the surface) whereas her chest and right arm, farther away in mid-ground, are blurred. This shot is particularly well-bungled as the selective focus that, logically, should have been established on Betty's face, is thwarted at the last second when the young woman turns her head... The shot is failed because the instant captured was not the right one. This is indeed a strange consideration in painting which, usually, knows nothing other than the pose.

[14] "The author of *The Origin* of *the Work of Art* recognizes only two kinds of iconicity: either the reduplication of an originary sight (the case of the reproductive image) or an inaugural and originary presentation of a being, conceived as the ultimate horizon of a hermeneutic universe. However, the photographic image is neither the first nor the second: we have seen that it is irreducible to any reduplicating function, but it is neither an originary emergence, because it is always caused by 'real' physical objects that are often already invested with specific hermeneutic functions. It is always the image of some thing, and is as such, somehow 'second.' But this 'secondariness' is unrelated to an originary sight: nothing prevents the photographic image from being unprecedented despite the fact that it is founded on 'beings' given in advance." Jean-Marie Schaeffer, op. cit., p. 17.

[15] With perhaps the exception of *studie* Zu *324 (Freud), 1971/323 1.2.3* and *Studie Zu 324*, 1971, as well as a few landscapes such as *Parkstück* already mentioned.

Mourning Photography

Again, the initial double-take is born of a contradiction between seeing photographs and knowing that they are oils on canvas. Unlike what one may feel before a hyperealist painting to which, in the end, there is not a whole lot more than dexterity with a paintbrush, the troubling aspect of Richter's paintings comes from the fact that, beyond the successful "simulation", one discovers visual anomalies that can only belong to photography (blur, "filé", "bougé", under and over exposure, etc...). In truth, Richter's *propos* would have quickly worn out if it were not a question, in each case, of painting failed shots or bungling photographs made of paint. Moreover, if photography is really a print and an *index,* that, according to Pierce, is a sign that refers to the object it denotes because it really is affected by that object[16], then the object, permeating the photograph, reaches its full existence and substantiality when it is imprinted on the film in the highest definition;[17] which goes to show how important it is for a photograph to be sharp and clear in order not to be a failed shot in the strongest sense of the word. For blurred outlines are the traces of a disappearing substance or of the beginning of the absence of the object that has left its mark. It is quite another story for the practice of painting which begins with the formless to reach form. When it starts to bring forth a figure in pictoral matter on the canvas, it is always something like the effect of a miracle; out of formless Ether or indistinct nebulae comes a presence — divine, which is why painting, in the specificity of its process, was religious art *par excellence,* the art of the Mystery of Creation that it mimed. If the figures of beings or things in painting can take forms that are not yet wholly defined, it is because they are

[16] See. Pierce: *Collected Papers,* vol.2, French tr. Deledalle, p. 123 [paraphrased back into English directly from the French translation, Tr.].

[17] The highest definition one could dream of, of course, because what we are dealing with is an analog photographic image. "The ideal limit of the phototonic image is no other than the mathematical image, a point to point mapping such that for every point of the imprinter there is a single and corresponding point in the print and vice versa. Jean-Marie Schaeffer, op. cit., p. 17.

beginning to become. A blur of outline here is no sign of loss of substance or of alteration but rather a promise of (be)coming, of bodying forth from the void, a sign that incarnation is almost achieved. What Richter nevertheless persists in painting are bungled photographs and even more often, he bungles photographs made of paint (when the photographs he works from are sharp).[18] It is certainly as though painting could no longer represent without referring to photographic images but even more as though painting provided the means to explore photography's margins and limits, as if it appropriated its singular modes of representation, redefined their specificity, and in the process of doing so uncovered its own power in what photography lacks[19]. What becomes strikingly apparent here is that the images of poor quality that we discover in Richter's painting would not at all retain our attention if they were just bad photographs, on the contrary, they affect us and retain our gaze the way painting does (*Gegenüberstellung, 1988/671* 1. 2. 3 [ill. 19]; *Tote 1988/667* 1. 2; *Festnahme* (1. 2), *1988/674* 1. 2). A word needs to be said here about the materiality of the photographic apparatus which, as Jean-Marie Schaeffer stresses, produces a sort of image that is always traversed by the "thesis of existence." Photography, effectively, "not only refers to real existences, as painting can also do (in particular, by way of a title, for instance: the *Arnolfini* portrait), it records their actual trace in a field of perception that, granted, is virtual, but that is nevertheless situated in a very real moment of space-time."[20] Richter's three *Gegenüberstellung,* presented quite clearly as three separate snapshots, are also traversed by the "thesis of existence", not by way of of a title or a context (which, most frequently, can not be determined) but by virtue of the visual nature of these images. Despite the fact that these are blurred or failed photographs that flaunt the traces of a

[18] See. *Sekretärin,* 1964; *Familie am Meer,* 1964/35; *Reisebüro,* 1966, etc.
[19] This is no longer the practice of painting that, at the beginning of the 20th century, was obliged to redefine its specificity — which was to be Abstraction — next to photography which was taking charge of representation. This is more the practice of painting that inaugurates its research by integrating photography.
[20] Jean-Marie Schaeffer, op. cit., p. 17.

loss of substance or the beginnings of absence, these works affect us, strangely enough, as "true" paintings, by inverting the image process in the field of photographic visibility itself. They do so by commuting photographic traces of disappearance into pictoral traces of apparition, by contrasting the figure fraying in the depth of an indistinctly gray pictoral space with the same figure that emerges on the surface of the canvass, thus painting's beginnings are superimposed on photography's death.

To be perfectly clear, the work of mourning is double. It concerns not only the content but also the nature of the image, the nature of its expression. First, concerning the contents of the image: these three snapshots are failed as to exposure, shutter speed and depth of field. These defects, as we have noted, alter the indexical inscription of the figure, it is a loss of substance that adds to the death-bearing character of the photograph, which is always the trace of a real and fleeting space-time that has passed. As for the nature of the image and its expression, if we had been confronted with the concrete reality of three shots of this quality, we would have identified them in a museum context as photo-documents not meant to be looked at in the long and contemplative way we look at painting. Such that this young woman is already in the process of disappearing, her contours and the opaqueness of her flesh are being eroded, the snapshots that show her already belong to the anonymous mass of press and other photo-archives that, by status, function and visual quality are meant to supply news and information networks. Yet these shots can not be likened to so many other photographs that are more or less anecdotal, spectacular, violent or tragic, in that they hold our gaze and work on this double task of mourning, mourning the young woman whose death comes to us as a presentiment, and mourning the snapshot itself that is incapable and powerless to have the same effect on us.

Thus it is in fact an understatement to assert that painting rediscovers its power by exploring the photographic image and its margins. Painting, must I say again, is a sign of essence: "In the appropriate context, a sign of essence can, without the slightest problem, refer to a specific object. Such that a pictoral portrait generallyrefers to the person it represents: from this point of view, it can fulfill the same function as the photographic portrait. Nonetheless, considered as a sign *in se,* it remains a sign of essence even when the referential and individualizing relation is perfectly well established. Inversely, a photographic image remains a sign of existence, even when it becomes impossible to establish the identity of the person pictured."[21] Working towards the definition and emergence of form in a formless substance, the entire process of painting tends toward apparition. Here, however, the image made of paint did not have its beginnings in the formless, it is constructed after another form that is both pre-established and existing, the photographic image, and it affirms the fullness of its moment in the void as well as the loss of substance established by the snapshot. Painting thus suspends the death-bearing movement of an unsuccessful photograph, it converts, as we have said, the extinction of the figure into resistance to disappearance, painting firmly plants the persistence of this young woman's figure on the immortal horizon it has always promised.

But it is not just in the phenomenological domain that Richter's practice of painting rediscovers its force. The young woman is in fact deceased as are all the people that appear in this series of paintings. And not without reason, she was a member of the

---

[21] Jean-Marie Schaeffer, op. cit., p. 122-123.

Baader-Meinhof group and the snapshots from which the artist painted are confidential documents from secret police archives. They are traces of the dark and troubled moments in German democracy of the 70s, the photographs themselves face oblivion and destruction. So the practice of painting here is not only a phenemenological resistance to extinction, it takes up political resistance to censorship. After all, it is more difficult to sequester images belonging to the art world and signed by a recognized artist than it is to destroy secret documents in police archives. But it is not a question of contenting oneself with circulating and publishing images hitherto unseen, that would be no better than an additional escalation in the process of turning the world into a spectacle. It is a question of transforming the nature of the image so that it can acquire, outside of the news media, the gravity of remembrance and the constructed depth of affect. This is where the phenomenological and the political stakes are indissolubly bound in Richter's work, the first begetting the necessity of the second. So painting is once again invested with the supreme function of *iconic consecration,* no longer the art of official history or hagiography, but interpretive and dissident. It leaves a trace and bears witness to History within the history of art, now commuting the precarious and fleeting character of blind news to the remembrance of History returned to vision.

Variations in Gray

"L'ennui de toute peinture est le gris." Delacroix

The first gray paintings appeared as early as the end of the 60s when Richter had for a long time "painted photographs" in black and white in which gray could only have been a major given. Yet when he got to these resolutely gray and non figurative works, this was taken as eclecticism and attached to the 20th century monochrome tradition.[22] In the gray paintings it is nonetheless difficult not to see a prolongation of pictoral research founded on and oriented toward the photographic image and apparatus, and particularly the notion of medium gray that is at the heart of photographic technique and of the chemical and physical standardization of printing.

Medium gray is equal parts black and white and is located at an equal distance on the gray scale between pure white and pure black, it reflects only eighteen per cent of the light it receives. The importance of this normative technical standard is that it is the reference for the photocells that measure light to allow setting the speed and aperture so that the refracted light is distributed in such a way that restitutes mean visibility.

During Richter's first black and white figurative period, he painted urban structures (*Stadtbild D, F, 1968/176.177 1*; *Stadtbild Paris, 1968/175*, [ill. 4], etc.) that seem to tend toward the homogeneity of medium gray.[23] The photographic references were aerial

[22] Those who took this as eclecticism include the artist himself in a 1986 conversation with Benjamin Buchloh, one of the historians most attentive to Richter's work (translated into English from the French translation]: "*Gerhard Richter:* the gray paintings, yes, I did them at a time when there were already monochromes everywhere. I painted them anyway. *Benjamin Buchloh:* Who are you thinking of when you say that they were everywhere? Klein? Kelly? *G.R.* No, not of Kelly, but of Bob Ryman, Brice Marden, Alan Charlton, Yves Klein and many others.*B.B.* Paraphrase as strategy, were you conscience of that? *G.R.*Not really didn't even consider the fact that that might have something eclectic about it. *B.B.* And nonetheless history leaves you no other choice than to be eclectic. *G.R.* I don't know, actually I don't think so. (...) Why then would I have gone to so much trouble to produce such diversity? *B.B.* Because you intend to declaim the inventory of every aspect, because for you it's a matter of painting's rhetoric and simultaneously of analysing that rhetoric." *Gerhard Richter,* op. cit. note 7, volume 2, Essays by Benjamin Buchloh.

[23] See. also sky series from the blurriest to the sharpest as to the definition of forms but tending, nonetheless, toward a homogeneity of light in the making of a medium gray in painting. (*Zeichnung,* 1989 *1, 2,* ; *Tourist (mit zwei Löwen), 1975/369*; *Tourist (mit ein Löwen) 1975/370*).

views whose definition is always compromised by the gray haze that characterizes cities especially when the rooftops are in zinc.... And for these paintings, the painter seemed only to use black and white paint, letting the brush "haphazardly" contaminate the black by the white and vice versa, until, in the indecision of architectural contours and the mixing of colors, a mean luminosity emerged that depended on the quantities of black and white that Richter had used. It was time to explore this technical photographic norm in a more radical fashion either by painting photographs or by painting paintings.... For painting photographs, medium gray became the initial norm from which to grade light intensities and the photographed portraits he produced (with "the right settings for the shot") simulated, on the normative scale of gray, the nature of the photographic imprint that proceeds from the crystallization of an emulsion (*Achtundvierzig Portraits*, *1972/324* 1. *48*). Or, on the contrary, medium gray became a monochrome threshold beneath which he painted non-figurative paintings and continued to mix equal quantities of black and white at length and with unbridled gestures on the very surface of the canvas (*Vermalung (Grau)*, *1972/ 326* 1. 2. 3. 5 [ill. 10]) to reveal within the gray scale, the nature of the pictoral imprint that proceeds by strokes, layers and overlapping.

Starting with medium gray to "paint photographs" or remaining below a medium gray threshold to "paint paintings" is to propose another pictorality for black and white and consequently for gray. Within the practice of painting, Richter confronts images that would seem to be the effect of photographic crystallization with what would seem to be their own deconstruction into the luminous intensities of pictoral matter. The artist begins with an exposure meter and ends up composing and decomposing a new and singular materialization of light in painting.

But Richter does not only mix black and white paint below a monochrome gray threshold, he also paints paintings that are "all" gray (*Grau*, 1970/*247* *1. 2. 3. 4* [ill. 7]), reminding us of Kodak's 8" x 10" neutral gray card that is used to check exposure meters or to take light readings for scenes particularly difficult to photograph. The change in perception provoked by changing scale and enlarging Kodak's card to 200 x 150 cm or 300 x 250 cm (*Grau* 1972/*334* *1.2.3.4.5*, 1973/*349*) would by no means justify Richter's monochrome production if the monochromes did not also provide the opportunity to explore the immediate vicinity of medium gray, and, above all, to experiment with the phenomenon of light absorption and reflection, unlike Kodak's famous gray card whose sole purpose is to reflect exactly eighteen per cent of the light it receives. When Richter does not limit himself to a semi-mechanical or industrial application of color *(Zwei Grau nebeneinander,* 1966/*143* *1* or *Drei Grau übereinander,* 1966/*143* *2)* the diverse ways he applies the paint, of weaving or even, say, of modeling the pictoral matter of these medium grays on the surface of the canvas, produces, in the process, infinite variations in the reflection and the absorption of light (*Grau* *1. 2. 3. 4*, etc. 1970) that activate, multiply or neutralize the light's points and angles of incidence on the painted surface of the canvas to the point of complete matteness or reflection (*Spiegel,* 1981/*485*, 1986/*619*; *Spiegel, grau, 1991/735* *1. 2. 3* [ill. 7]). So Richter sets out to mix and combine brilliance and matteness, to take every liberty in experimentation and manifest in paint all the nuances of expression possible within the parameters of photography's extremely normative and technically limited optical vocabulary.

Democracy is Medium Gray

What is at stake is much more than craft and a willful multiplication of phenomenological experiments with light, that would be a kind of endless inventory whose value, again, would be short lived. Learning and discovering the possibilities of painting within photography's vocabulary also means taking a critical stance toward this vocabulary, finding a political position and making a commitment that is, once again, indissociable from a phenomenological position. If Richter himself effectively feels that despite his research in and around medium gray, the gray monochromes express "indifference, lack of conviction and a refusal to make any sort of commitment at all," then we have every reason to believe there might be something suspicious about the extreme standardization imposed by "the gray card" on the visibility of the world, when amateur photographers and photo-journalists are led to grade reality in luminosity. Richter gives us the opportunity to experience this for ourselves in movement and on a one to one scale. In applying a uniform gray to a canvas 280 x 165 cm and covering this with a pane of glass (*Spiegel, grau,* 1991), he has given viewers the chance to contemplate themselves as in a full length mirror and to discover virtual images of themselves moving across a median light area on the scale of gray but it is also the opportunity to despair over the missing colors and forms as well as that part of the light that has been occulted.

It is probably no coincidence that several gray monochromes are entitled *Spiegel* (see. 1981, 1986, etc.), a word signifying mirror but that also designates the largest German daily, *Der Spiegel.* Such that it is not only a question of denouncing the visibility of the world photographic standards afford us, but also of denouncing the comprehensibility of the world as pictured in the paper. Mallarmé described newspapers in these terms* "Sheet spread, full, (that) borrows from printing an unwarranted result, of simple mackling (...) sheet ready, as it has received the imprint, showing to the first degree, raw, the flow of a text"[24]. It is tempting to read into this white sheet of paper mackled with black ink the emergence of a medium gray as image and sign of some "medium meaning" given by the paper. And it would seem that newspapers are, in fact, highly emblematic of our immediate reading of the world in Western democratic societies. They are even the principle vehicles for the words and images into which our local and planetary environment are put; newspapers compose and officiate the daily social mass of which Hegel spoke; they attempt to be the ideally universal and singular tools of an opinion at once free and common, in which each of us would discover the world and our thoughts on the world and so share with each other, in consensus, the most common opinion. Newspapers are then quintessential places of democracy where we would all have, to paraphrase Adorno on the United States, the liberty to see and think like everybody else. Richter's work on monochrome gray outfits phenomenological resistance as much as it constructs political dissent. Resistance, in modeling this "color" on the flat canvas to explore the limitless and specific resources with which painting can model light; dissent, when he designates medium gray as the

---

[24] Mallarmé, *Le Livre, instrument spirituel,* Gallimard, La Pléiade (1945), p.379-380. *"Feuille étalée, pleine, (qui) emprunte a l'impression un résultat indu, de simple maculature (...) feuille à même, comme elle a reçu empreinte, montrant au premier degré, brut, la coulée d'un texte."* The translation of this excerpt of the poem is purely referential and by no means accounts for Mallarmé's use of language that constructs meanings in unusual ways. For instance, here, emprunte (borrow), a homonym of empreinte (imprint, print, track, mark, stamp, etc.), is thus linked through sound to *l'impression* (printing, impression), such that what "to borrow" and "to print" have in common, taking (shape) something from someone or something else, stands out. This language is and isn't referential in the same way that Kandinsky's Abstract Composition #2 is and isn't figurative. Mallarmé taught English and it is not impossible that in *feuille étalée* he was also, but not only, thinking of the English term "spread sheet." {Tr.]

optical and cognitive destiny of our democracies to the extent that seeking the largest common denominator of visibility for images and of legibility for texts, appears ever more threateningly, as our totalitarian horizon.[25]

Clouds

It would certainly not be out of bounds to see in Richter's paintings of clouds (see. *Wolken 1970/265, Wolke, 1970/270 1. 2. 3* [ill.8]) the origin of his abstract paintings that become more and more frequent after the the first *Abstraktes Bild* in 1976. There is quite a paradox in representing blurry clouds when they are the only motif in the image, from both pictoral and photographic points of view. In the practice of painting, where the notion of blurriness doesn't exist, the sky, much less the heavens, are not painted for themselves, even if wisps of clouds allow veiling the light, the *sfumato* or atmospheric haze that results always bathes or troubles the contours of earthly forms (mountains, forests, buildings, people....), so much does light in sacred art remain the symbolic and significant link between heaven and earth as well as, for the 19th century Impressionists, the phenomenon that allows form to appear. In contrast, the notion of blurriness is technically consubstantial with photography. To photograph an object is to measure its distance from the lens with accuracy, to focus on it means relegating the space behind, before or around it to blurriness depending on the lens being used (fisheye, wide angle, telephoto lens, etc.). And though clouds can more readily than in painting constitute the sole motif in the frame, their status is singular in that, as far as depth of field is concerned, they are both

---

[25] The injunctions of the "politically correct" order that has prevailed in the United States over the last ten years is quite symptomatic of a trend in Western democracies not to take political positions through decision-making authorities but rather to practice and encourage, in searching for the largest possible concensus among social forces, what Virilio calls "social cybernetics." This is all well and good for the liberal economy that works to produce and circulate products, images and texts that are as universal as money and God.

figure and background.[26] The way they are shot is global and the optical sharpness of their contours is to some extent "natural."[27]

When Richter decides to paint blurry clouds in and for themselves, the image is no less paradoxical in painting than it is in photography. There is more to it however, the motif, treated in this fashion, contributes to the emergence of abstract forms in an optical space. These clouds without sky or earth are a source of innumerable images that, moreover, always appear far off in the field of perception, they are never something one might touch but are a motif of distance, a fact that permits the painter to compose, and this is the ultimate paradox, abstract paintings in photographic space (see. *Fiktion* 1975/372 4, *Wolke* 1976/414, *Abstraktes Bild* 1977/428, *idem* 1978/437), which is to say to paint nonfigurative forms with no referent in spaces that are by nature indexical spaces of existing forms.

It would seem to me that this, for Richter, is the frame in which his work on abstraction has developed. The first abstract forms (1976-1977), however painterly, unfurl across faraway, "sidereal," spaces without anything that would give viewers a notion of direction or scale and in which the light, soft or violent, seems more electric than natural (see. *Abstraktes Bild* 1977/429. 430). But when the artist adds geometric planes, they are by no means a function of the concrete flatness of the canvas as the neoplastic tradition of our century would have it, but rather, they are volumes (irregular polyhedrons) (see. *Merlin* 1982/519, *SDI* 1986/ 590) or even float in an optical space into which they introduce, through fissures, cracks and windows, other spheres of the space (see. *Konstruction* 1976/389, *Abstraktes Bild* 1977/422.424). Once these optical spaces no longer index existing forms that belong to

---

[26] It is moreover impossible to imagine seeing the enlarged detail of a cloud. Trying to enlarge a detail would mean getting lost in its indeterminate water vapour.

[27] If clouds, as the sole motif of the image, are finally blurred in photography, this is because the focus has voluntarily been set on a (terrestrial) foreground, necessarily outside the frame.

an originary reality, then they no longer refer to photographic images but to another kind of image, born on the computer screen, an optical space of a virtual nature, where worlds of abstract forms nest, collapse and open one into the other. If the photographic image thus nourishes Richter's new phenomenological field, it would also seem that computer images nourish his abstract painting, indifferently painterly or geometric. The first is an anolog language and the second a digital language but fundamentally they share the same optical space of expression. Nevertheless, in neither case does the artist renounce the haptic dimension of his painting (see. the exemplary portraits of the Bakers, 1965). Once again, he brings the immaterial forms of optical space into confrontation with pictoral forms that have a thickness, that express proximity, tactility and the prevalence of colored substances, forms that inscribe the artist's wide and unbridled movements across the surface of the canvas (see. *SDI* 1986/590, *Abstraktes Bild* (Grün) 1986/588 *1.2.3*).

The haptic dimension of Richter's work asserts itself with more insistence in the abstract canvasses. This concrete and painterly work on the surface of the canvas is always gestural and expressionist, that is, if one wishes to situate it in a tradition, an act which is hardly innocent. Compared to geometric abstraction, pictoral events are effectively more singular in the sense that the idiosyncrasy of the strokes at any given moment make the resulting shapes and textures more difficult to copy or duplicate. And the latter do not appear in isolation on the surface of a blank canvas, but on the surface of a painting comprising an optical space that is already swimming with shapes, light and opacities that refer to computer generated images. This optical space and its images that occupy the canvas like a pre-existing ground, whatever their complexity, develop and can be translated into a digital language that assures infinite duplication. It is on the surface of these digital images and not on the surface of a blank canvas that Richter begins to paint his expressionist paintings *(Abstraktes Bild* (Grün) 1986/588 *1.2.3, SDI* 1986/590), as if what he required were not blank canvasses but computer screens continuously radiating light and shapes. What comes out of this work, particularly between 1978 and 1986, is a strong and even violent tension between an optical space of the kind provided by the computer screen and the haptic space of pictoral images. The latter make an attempt to coat and occult the radiant ground, the canvas becomes a space for confrontation between images of two different natures. The painter is careful not to attempt to arbitrate the encounter and works, on the contrary, to make the confrontation all the more visible. The experience this confrontation provides and the questions it raises belong to the pictoral domain because they allow painting to manifest its phenomenological power to contain and bring forth, simultaneously, two heterogeneous worlds of imagery. Painting reaffirms its importance, not by restricting its specificity and losing ground to other image media but by doing just the opposite, by expanding to integrate them into its own processes of expression.

Video Painting

Each time Richter ventures into new ways of painting based on an approach to other image media, his research nonetheless continues to develop as a coherent whole. His visual propositions unfold along side one another but in a reciprocal perspective through which they exchange the concepts and share the questions that progressively constitute the weight and unity of the oeuvre. Such is the figurative worked inspired by photographic images, the gray monochrome work that came out of the way photography measures light, and the abstract work suggested just as much by synthesized images as by "clouds" in painting or photography. We could have made more attentive references to newspapers and to offset techniques, to the color charts used by printers (see. *Farben 1974/352* 1. 2. 3. 4 [ill. 13]), to the pixelization of television and computer screens (see. *1024 Farben, 1974/355* 1.2, *1024 Farben, 1974/358* 1.2, *4096 Farben, 1974/359*), all pertinent to this painter's research that coils in and around our technical and technological times to nourish itself with the emergence of new image phenomenologies. But I will conclude this study with an analysis of the many large scale paintings of the last six years (see. *Abstraktes Bild, Brick Tower* 1987/643 1. 2. 3. 4. 5) *Abstraktes Bild* 1990/726; *Bach* 1992/785; *Abstraktes Bild* 1993/794 1.2.3, etc.) that will permit me to speak of a kind of amalgamation of optic and haptic images, made possible by a new painting technique that produces a visual scrambling effect, as if colors and forms were flitting across a canvas-screen at top speed. The artist uses boards as large scrapers or squeegees to spread thicknesses of paint in the nearly uniform layers that, together with the optical forms, compose the painting. It is almost like a glaze, most often applied in horizontal strokes, that melds expressionist and optical images in such a way that through the thick glazing still shine and radiate the immaterial and readily vertical optical shapes in silhouette (*Abstraktes Bild* 1990/726, *idem.* 1991/747 1.2.3, *idem.* 1992/780). In this way, the tension that was previously made visible in the stratification and superimposition of images comes to a sort of resolution in a lateral sweep that operates a physical and pheno-menological crunch and mixing of two different worlds. This technique, that would seem to achieve the amalgamation, or better, the osmosis of haptic and optic images, essentially proceeds through the movement that it transmits to the surface of the canvas and in so doing conjures another medium: video. Indeed, the composition in lateral layers of pictoral materials that jam and scramble the vertical images of light produces the visual sensation of a video still that has become illegible because the tape is being played too rapidly, and sometimes there is the sensation of the camera panning or swooping sideways too rapidly and too close. In working on the direction and diffraction of form and color, on the flickering quality of luminous frequencies and the osmosis of two different worlds of image through lateral play and sweep, Richter integrates the phenomenological field of video into his painting. Yet the smoothing of the surface of the canvas-screen is haphazard enough that the layers of paint retain in their thickness the tactile qualities of a rotting, peeling, blistered, old wall that has acquired a patina (see. *November* 1989/701), or of an even, fine, soft and supple skin, or of a toughened hide torn and shredded in places (see. *Abstraktes Bild* 1990/722 *2. 3*), or even the surface of water rippled by the wind (see. *Wald, 1990/731 1. 2. 3. 4* [ill. 23]), all of which confers on these video images the density, materiality, coloring and fluidity that are painting's own. *Wald,* exemplary in this respect, is a painting I would not hesitate to call "video water lilies" as Richter's four paintings suddenly remind me of Monet.

In the indifference that video shows to the contents of its own images,[28] — that in these paintings fleet by illegibly — Richter

[28] Video can receive and transmit both sound and visual signals as well as both kinds of images, analog or digital. But as a *productive activity is* not at the level of input or reception but its output or transmission. It is enough that the connections are turned on and the lines plugged in, that electronic signals circulate, that figures cross the screen because "the representation no longer refers to a distinct object but to the productive activity itself," says Deleuze. Video clips are in this respect exemplary as neither figure nor sound exists in and for itself as an object. The connection and the fact that figures and sounds quickly follow one upon the other with neither syntax nor story are enough to assure that the clip is doing its job, which is to say, filling.../...

discovers the specific quality of video light and optical radiation on the scale of wall or fresco while giving them the haptic presence of paint. As for the practice of painting, it discovers a new vocabulary and particularly a new expression of the notion of blurriness, unrelated to photography's motionless measure of depth of field, blur as the effect of the frames speeding across the screen. Painting also discovers the need for its existence, for it to be the persistence of skin and the resistance of matter that cannot be translated or recycled into an optical video space that would make painting into a reproducible electromagnetic image that is placeless and astray in the anonymous entropy of electric image networks.

In this fashion, Richter unceasingly tests painting's *tolerance* to a world and to image media that are ever more universal and planetary and that seem, quite naturally, to sketch and resketch the death of painting on the horizon.

Painting meets its renaissance in Richter's work not because the painter's skill makes it so capable of simulating other media, but because it develops a greater perceptive intelligence of optical, analog and digital images. Moreover, in the margins and technical limits of other media, painting finds something for itself: forms of visibility that allow it both to make new phenomenological pro-positions and to found political position and commitment. Painting is then no longer a medium that has retreated into the enclave of reflexivity, it has a new transitive access to the world and to History.

This is why, in my opinion, Richter's painting can by no means be apprehended as a combination or eclectic paraphrase of

.../... the screen and saturating the air with sound until the next clip. "No aspect of the flow, not sound, image, gesture, etc., is priveleged in this language that remains indifferent to its substance and to its support as amorphous continuum; the electronic flow can be considered as the realization of any kind of flow as such." (Deleuze Guattari, *L'anti-Œdipe,* Paris, Minuit, coll. Critique, 1975, p.286. Also consult, on Sigmar Polke: Luc Lang, "*La peinture et l'électricité*", in *Peinture, Emblèmes et Références,* CAPC Bordeaux, 1993.) Here Richter rightly does without an actual Visualization of video images, he retains the quality of the radiation, movement and flickering of their luminous waves.

all 20th century forms of painting. This is not an oeuvre that belongs to the history of painting, it is one that participates in today's story of the image for which *Abstraktes Bild* would be the emblematic and obsessional statement: Richter does not paint paintings he paints images.

Photography, Painting and the Real
The Question of Landscape in the Painting of Gerhard Richter

*I want to make a photograph.*G. R.

*B*y setting out to consider the role of landscape in Gerhard Richter's painting, one runs a double risk. The first has to do with the by now anachronistic character of the category of "landscape painting": it has been a good while since the term, like "history painting," has been socially effective in defining an artistic project. The second has to do with the painter's œuvre itself. The variety of Richter's work, of which landscapes make up only one part (about a tenth, according to the painter's own estimate in 1985, with a diminishing proportion since then)[1] seemingly denounces the narrowness of such a project. In an œuvre where paintings resembling photographs coexist with *abstract* paintings, one which not only visits different *genres* but also puts into practice within them various modes of treating the material, each quite heterogeneous, can landscape be anything more than a simple and ironic take on an obsolete genre, the local and happenstance vehicle of a proposition that goes far beyond it?

[1] Interview with Dorothea Dietrich, March 5, 1985, *The Print Collector's Newsletter* # 4, september 9, 1985, p. 128.

This initial misconception would be all the more serious as the artist himself has repeatedly warned us of the futility and risk involved in dividing up his work into plots that can be only too easily cultivated: "For me there is no difference between a landscape and an abstract painting.... I refuse to limit myself to one option — to an external resemblance or a unity of style that can never exist.... A color table [ill. 13] can only be differentiated from a small green landscape from the outside [ill. 16]. They both reflect the same basic position. It is that position which is important."[2]

Though it may not be embodied in a particular image or category of images, or even in a particular genre or gestural mode in painting, this position emerges very forcefully in the constant relationship Richter's work maintains with photography.[3]

This takes a double form. The first is the production of series of paintings done from photographs, the series themselves divisible into, on one hand, paintings which mimic the look of a photographic image and its reality effect, and on the other, paintings which also begin with a photographic projection but nonetheless insist on their own materiality, drawing the image toward abstraction.

The second great series is the *abstract* paintings [ill. 23, 25], to which may be added the the group of paintings that have been

[2] Interview with Irmeline Lebeer, *L'art vivant*, February, 1973, p. 15. This fundamental non-differentiating cannot be ascribed exclusively to a willfulness on the part of the artist. "Experience has shown me that there is no difference between a painting one calls realist— a landscape, for example—and an abstract one; *they have about the same effect on the viewer.*" (*Ibid.*) And elsewhere: "How do you see your work? Is it divided into groups, or are these different aspects of one and the same thing?" "I think it's a question of different aspects of one thing, which one can always divide up or classify. One may, if you will, create many drawers, for smaller paintings, large-scale ones, the middle-sized ones, figurative ones, colored paintings, and those in black and white... But it always comes down to one and the same thing: finding out how to deal, in this world, with myself and with painting." Interview with Jonas Storsve, *La peinture à venir* ("Painting to Come"), *Art Press*, # 161 (September 1991), p. 20.

[3] This may go so far as to take the form of a denial. See below, note 78.

called *constructivist* [ill. 12]. These paintings, by virtue of their name as well as their visually anti-representational look, seem to validate analyses which make abstraction into a product of the revolution in art wrought by photography. The latter having taken over the realm of description, which until then was the task of painterly imitation, painting itself had to settle for the possibility of abstraction and modernism. Richter himself accepts this analysis in part. "One can hardly speak of photography as such any more," he has declared, "for it is obvious that it has taken over an important part of painting: description and representation. This has modified painting considerably."[4]

As we can see, the abstract paintings find their support in photography as much as the photo-paintings do. It is in this dialectical relationship of both of them to photography that, even before going on to the question of landscape proper, we can isolate an underlying "basic" position.

Photography, Art, Reality

Photography became established in Richter's work in several stages. At the end of the' 50s, and with the goal of escaping the images and problematics of the art history, he began using photographs to establish the visual content of his paintings. Starting in 1962, the photographs, previously limited to furnishing "non-artistic" *themes*, become, in the very way they *look*, visual models

[4] For an even more radical affirmation of this view, see Richter's recent interview with Henri-François Debailleux: "I can do abstract painting in a quasi-professional manner. With the figure, on the other hand, this is almost impossible. There is no room for chance. You also need a very special angle and conditions—and even those you have to be able to find—because *since it has come into existence, photography has forbidden practically everything*". "Montrer ce que je veux" ("Showing what I wish"), *Libération*, October 5, 1993. Richter does not see this transformation as exclusively a consequence of the *technical invention* of photography: "The fact that painting has changed is not due only to the invention of photography. Music is familiar with those difficulties and is undergoing comparable transformations, enormous ones which do not have their origin in a technical invention." Storsve, *op. cit.*, p. 17.

for the work. Richter copied photographic prints: he projected photographs (almost exclusively black-and-white) onto the canvas and painted them in the tones of the original, after which "the contours were rubbed out with a dry brush, the whole thing becoming blurred and out of focus."[5] At first these were photographs from the news, rather rarely from advertising, taken from the current press. In the paintings, they were presented as is, occasionally with an accompanying caption. There were also amateur photographs, tourist and souvenir snapshots like those hidden away by the millions in family photo albums. In both cases, the choice was based on their ordinary character, the fact of their "visual indifference," in the sense that Duchamp demonstrated with the *readymades*.[6]

The coexistence of the news photographs with the amateur souvenir and album snapshots (and the increasing percentage of the latter), however, shows quite readily that unlike the Pop artists with whom he was first associated, what was at stake in the use of photography did not lie for Richter in its status as mechanical reproduction of the image or in its media-like existence.[7]

A primary expression of this difference is Richter's marginal interest, in silk-screen and other modern reproduction techniques, which he never employed in making his paintings, unlike Warhol

[5] Lebeer, *op. cit.*, p. 13.

[6] "There is one point that I wish to establish very clearly. The choice of the readymades was never dictated to me out of any esthetic delight. The choice was based on a reaction of visual indifference, accompanied at the time by a total lack of good or bad taste..., in fact a total anesthesia." Marcel Duchamp, "*À propos des readymades*," in *Duchamp du signe* (Paris, 1975), p. 191. On the relationship of the readymade to the photographic act, see Rosalind Krauss, "Notes on the Index," in *The Originality of the Avant-Garde and other Modernist Myths* (Cambridge, Mass. 1985). See also Benjamin H. D. Buchloh, "Readymade, photographie et peinture dans la peinture de Gerhard Richter," in *Gerhard Richter*, vol. II: *La peinture à la fin du sujet* [*Painting at the End of the Subject*] (Paris, 1993).

[7] See Sean Rainbird, "Variations on a Theme: The Paintings of Gerhard Richter," *Gerhard Richter*, Tate Gallery exhibition catalogue (London, 1991), p. 14. That Richter at one time flirted with a Pop identity is attested to by his visit to the Sonnabend Gallery in Paris in 1962, where, in the company of Konrad Lueg, he introduced himself as 'a German Pop artist.'"

and Rauschenberg. In addition, he never multiplied or super-imposed photographic images in the same painting.[8] Finally, if a Pop logic, more specifically a Warhol-like one in its obsession with death, may still have dominated the choice of images used in the first photo-paintings (1962–1963), the increasing proportion of anonymous and ordinary snapshots indicated that he had gone beyond it towards a broader set of issues, going back to one of Duchamp's original speculations: the possibility of "making works that are not 'of art' come from art."[9]

To Richter's own surprise, it was photography that embodied this possibility:

> Photography, which we all use so frequently, surprised me. I was suddenly able to see it in a different way, as an image that transmitted a different look, without the conventional criteria that I used to attach to art. There was no style, no composition, no judgment. It liberated me from personal experience. There was nothing but a pure image. As a result, I wished to possess it and represent it — not to use it as a means for painting, but to use painting as a means for photography.[10]

By short-circuiting style, composition and judgment, photography gives rise to something these three elements were an obstacle to: an image of the real stripped of any will to art.[11] Or rather, it indicates the approximation of greatest verisimilitude to certain conditions, clarified by Richter's photographic choices. The amateur or family photographs he chooses in fact share several presuppositions, which can be combined into a basic position. The first is that in shooting, the automatism of the machine takes precedence over any possible artistic intentions on the part of the operator. From this point of view, photography is an "art without

[8] Of the Pop artists, Richter is closest to Lichtenstein, also a painter of one image per painting. In other respects the latter's "anti-pictural technique, directed against painting," was also more attractive to him. See "Réception de l'avant-garde 1986," in Buchloh, *op. cit.*, p. 94.

[9] Marcel Duchamp, *A l'infinitif*, in *op. cit.*, p. 105.

[10] Interview with Rolf Schön, *Gerhard Richter*, exhibition catalogue, 1972 Venice Biennale, p. 23.

[11] "I became interested in photography because it illustrates [*abbildet*] reality so well." Interview with Rolf Günther Dienst, *ibid.*, p. 20.

an artist."[12] The second is a conception of a "good photo" that can be summed up in a double demand: that one recognize what is being represented, and that the intervention of the overall apparatus not trouble the transparency of this recognition. The final presupposition is that amateur photographs capture only that which is already "photographable": family, loved ones, travels, visits, etc.[13] It is this basic position that Richter's selection of photographic material both vouches for and claims.[14] Quite logically, during the late 60s Richter himself started taking "ordinary" photographs which he made into material for his images. It is this procedure he now uses exclusively for all his figurative paintings.[15]

It would be wrong to interpret this move away from the use of "found" photos to ones taken by the artist himself as a return to subjective individual expression. Quite the contrary, the photo-

[12] "Nothing is more directly opposed to the general picture of artistic creation than the activity of the amateur photographer, who mostly asks the camera to do most of the operations for him or her, identifying the degree of perfection of the machine with how automatic it is." Pierre Bourdieu, *Un art moyen. Essai sur les usages sociaux de la photographie* (Paris, 1965), "Introduction," p. 23–24. The expression "art without an artist" occurs in chapter 2 of the book (*La définition sociale de la photographie*), in a similar context.

[13] Pierre Bourdieu, *op. cit.*, *Occasions de pratique et pratique d'occasion*, pp. 54–64. Bourdieu goes on to say, "Landscape photography differs little, from the point of view of its esthetic and its subjects, from family photography, except for the fact that it is more often in color, both because it is mostly done by people who are tourists and therefore in a better position to use this costly method, and because the color snapshot better fulfils the expectations of realism." *Ibid.*, p. 62, note.

[14] "Apparently banal photos are, quite the contrary, the richest ones... They have less of the 'snapshot' about them than any of the others. What else is there in this domain? Artistic photographs, composed. These are much more grievous artistic clichés, fundamentally impoverished images, with their play of light and shadow, harmony and compositional effects. *By comparison, the family photo, with everybody just standing here in the center of the image, is literally overflowing with life.*" Lebeer, *op. cit.*, p. 15 (emphasis mine). Elsewhere Richter declared, "Composition is completed when the principal character is put down in the center. That's it." Quoted by Klaus Honnef in *Gerhard Richter*, Venice Biennale, *op. cit.*, p. 15.

[15] The importance of this photographic material took public form with the exhibition and publication of *Atlas*, a set of plates excerpted from from these archives.

graphs taken by Richter, because of their subject-matter (private and family life, portraits, landscapes taken on trips) as well as their neutrality of composition, are in no way distinguishable from millions of others of the same type. Subjected to the rules of amateur photographic practice, the personal experience of the artist becomes as objectified and banal, by the same process and under the same conditions, as the others. Above and beyond the singularity of each image, it is the photographic material used by Richter as a whole that "gives itself over, manifestly and completely, to photographic practice, dissolves into it and seemingly lets itself be absorbed by it."[16]

By adopting the social criteria that regulate amateur photography and aggressively claiming its esthetic legitimacy, Richter does not, however, in spite of the occasional ambiguity of his positions, set one claim against another.[17] If the snapshots he chose to keep outline the contours of an opposition to the Beaux-Arts and academic tradition, their value as *something else* and the surprise caused by the photography are not basically a question of content. They stem from the apparatus itself. From this point of view, the act that established the ground for Richter's practice was the decision he made in 1962 to copy, in painting, the *look* of the photographic print. This decision to execute photographs in painting, far from simply referring to the climate in the early years of the 60s, is in fact a new way of coming to terms with the situation created in the first half of the nineteenth century by the invention of photography, and of the trauma it continues to inflict on painterly practice.

[16] See Benjamin H. D. Buchloh, *L'archive anomique de Gerhard Richter, op. cit.*, p. 16. One might liken this analysis to Polke and Richter's declaration in the catalogue of their joint exhibition in 1966: "I want to be like everybody, I want to think what everybody thinks, I want to do what is done anyway." Polke/Richter exhibition catalogue, Galerie h, (Hanover, 1966), quoted by Jürgen Harten, *Gerhard Richter: Bilder/Paintings 1962–1985* (Cologne, 1986), p. 57.

[17] See. Richter's declaration also in the text jointly written with Polke in 1966 : "I find many amateur photos better than the best Cézanne." *Ibid.*

Photography, Painting: Between Index and Analogy

The crisis brought about just before the middle of the nineteenth century by the appearance and rapid spread of photographic images was in fact above all that of the *destination* or
mission of painting as it had progressively defined itself since the
Renaissance. It was more precisely the "catastrophic" moment of
an ongoing crisis since the second half of the eighteenth century,
one which concerned the categories of imitation and representation. The growing ambition of conveying reality as is, in a
scientific manner, to describe *what is seen* with objectivity, called
into question the definition of the concepts which had ruled the
relationship of painting to objects and that of looking to the
visible. The increasing use of the *camera obscura* and the pro-
liferation, towards the end of the eighteenth and at the turn of the
nineteenth centuries, of apparatuses and systems used as mechanical aids for eye and hand are both symptomatic of this crisis.[18]
What these instruments shared in common was the devaluation of
the intervention of the hand and of the individual singularity of
the subject, the theoretical goal of the mechanization of the
process being the direct inscription of the real perceived in the
form of an image traced on a surface. The invention of photography is, in a certain sense, the culmination of this process.[19]
With it comes the total suppression of the hand, in the sense of
the hand of the artist. With it the mechanical lens of the camera
replaces the eye of the subject.

This invention, while a culmination, is at the same time the
inauguration of a new history. "The art of fixing a shadow," to
recall the wonderful definition of photography coined by Fox-

[18] For example Chrestien's *Physionotrace* or Wollaston's *Camera lucida*. See.
Jonathan Crary, *Techniques of the Observer: On Vision and Modernity in the
Nineteenth Century* (Cambridge, Mass., 1990). For an overview of these problems
see Roland Recht's suggestive *La lettre de Humboldt* (*The Letter from Humboldt*)
(Paris, 1989).
[19] See. Peter Galassi, *Before Photography: Painting and the Invention of Photography*
(New York, 1981), and particularly the critique of it proposed by Rosalind Krauss in
"Les espaces discursifs de la photographie," *Le Photographique* (Paris, 1990).

Talbot, by virtue of the specific genesis of its images, moves them from one signifying regime to another. In contrast to one practice of the image, painting, which until then primarily invoked the concept of imitation to achieve relationships of resemblance, photography distinguishes itself in radical fashion by the operation of chemical recording of the action of light, giving it the quality of a physical trace, an *index*. It becomes, to cite the definition of this concept given by Charles Sanders Peirce, "a sign which refers to the object it denotes because it is really affected by this object."[20] Even when there is an iconic, analogical resemblance, as is the case with most ordinary uses of the photographic image, it is its indexical character, not the iconic one, that gives the sign its specificity.[21]

The singular relationship that painting and photography sustain is grounded both in the indexical quality of photography, one which painting does not possess, at least when it is conceived as an imitative representation,[22] and in the fact that photography possesses, and here as much as painting, an iconic and analogical value. Because painting cannot make us believe in the real existence of what is shown in the image, and does not, in other words, have the same value in *recording the real* as photography, the latter can claim to surpass painting and discover better resemblances.[23] This was the surprise, horror or delight of the first practitioners and viewers of photography: it was a physical trace of objects (even at a distance), an index, and this index was *also*, given, it is true, a

[20] Quoted in Jean-Marie Schaeffer, *L'image précaire. Du dispositif photographique* (Paris, 1987), pp. 55–56.

[21] "To the extent that the index is affected by the object, it necessarily has some quality in common with it. and it in respect to these qualities that it refers to the object. It therefore implies a kind of icon, even though it is an icon of a particular kind. It is not the mere resemblance it has to the object, even in this respect, that makes it into a sign, but *its being truly changed by the object." Ibid.* (Emphasis mine.)

[22] Here I am speaking of painting "before photography." As we shall see later, and with Richter himself, modern painting, and more generally modern art, are marked by the indexical character of the work, and in a form quite different from the residual one of *style* or *manner*.

[23] See. Samuel Morse's dictum in 1840: "Daguerrotypes cannot be called copies of Nature; they are Nature itself."

certain loss of information (color, nuances in tone), a better imitation than the painted image. On the other hand, adversaries of photography, and partisans against it of painting, will highlight the loss of information, along with the absence of construction in the image. It is important to note that the debate is made possible not by the simple opposition between photography/index on the one hand and painting/icon on the other, but by the fact that in most ordinary uses of photography, it is the iconic-analogical value that takes over.[24] In this economy, the indexical character has a new function, that of authenticating the discourses which are based on the image and reinforcing their truth-value. The privilege accorded photography, the belief in its objectivity, essentially resides in the confusion — although normal enough, none the less real and sometimes organized — between its indexical value, which makes it into the necessary trace of an event or fact, and the ability imputed to it to authenticate the meaning of this event or fact. This ability implies the work of interpreting the image, for although the index tells us that something has happened, it does not tell us what.[25]

The indexical function of the photograph does not in fact reside in the appearance it takes on. For an image to be accorded the status of a photographic sign, it does not suffice, strictly speaking, for it to have the *look* of a photograph; one must be able to consider its *genesis* to have been produced by the photographic apparatus.[26] This, for example, is what distinguishes a digitalized image from a photograph, in spite of the possibility that they might be optically identical.[27] The practice of photography being

[24] From this point of view, it is far from insignificant that the first massive use of photography was in the *portrait* industry, formerly the specific object of painting. There the value of analogical resemblance is clearly predominant.

[25] See. Peirce: "Anything which focuses the attention is an index. Anything that startles us is an index, in so far as it marks the junction between two portions of experience. Thus a tremendous thunderbolt indicates that something considerable happened, although we may not know precisely what the event was." In *The art of reasoning*, chapter 2, in *Collected Papers*, vol. II, § 285, (Cambridge, Mass., 1932), p. 161.

[26] See. J.-M. Schaeffer, *op. cit., passim*.

[27] Here one can cite the work of someone like Jeff Wall, who, while using the resources of computers and digitalization, confronts the problems of composition and meaning in the 'great machines' of history painting in the nineteenth century.

well nigh universal, this form of knowledge is among the most widely shared throughout the world, and one may expect it of everyone. The fact remains that even if the look of a photograph leads us, out of visual or cultural habit, to expect the indexical character of the image, it remains insufficient, in and of itself, for guaranteeing this indexicality. A great number of ordinary uses of photography take advantage of this ambiguity. There the indexical character of the image takes on the role of an authenticating supplement for the discourse which is supported by the image/icon, but not inscribed in the image/index.

Painting Photos

After the appearance of the photographic apparatus, imitative painting and its primarily iconic mode of operation could no longer constitute a viable model for the fabrication of images; this is true even from the point of view of analogical resemblance. By painting/copying photographs, Richter takes a position in the debate that has opposed painting and photography, and he appears to resolutely take the side of the latter: "I have painted photos precisely in order not to have anything to do with *painting*; it constitutes an obstacle to any expression appropriate to our time.[28] Working by projecting the photographic print on the canvas with an overhead projector, in such a way as to preserve its *look* with the greatest amount of precision, Richter displays the subordination of painting with respect to the photographic mode.[29] However, the object produced is a contradictory one.

First of all, the means used to reproduce the photographic image are those of iconic imitation: once the photo is projected on

[28] Interview with Benjamin Buchloh, *op. cit.*, p. 94.
[29] Even here he goes back to an old practice. By the 1860s photographic enlargements were being either projected or printed on canvas, allowing the painter to produce works which, in the words of *Photographic News* of 1863, had all the merit of photographic exactitude. See Aaron Scharf, *Art and Photography*, p. 56–8.

the canvas, the painter traces its outlines in pencil. The photographic print is then meticulously copied in oil. There is a double irony here. The elements which have for centuries constituted the archetypal means of iconic imitation — line drawing and oil painting — are subordinated here to the imitation of that which ruined its calling, the photographic print. But there is no less an irony with respect to the latter: by reconstituting the photographic look with traditional means, Richter empties the image produced of its indexical character, that is, of its only claim to supersede painting as a good recording of the real.

This irony is worked not so much on the indexical character of the photograph as on its usual link to the icon and its role as "authenticating" supplement, which it calls into question.[30]

> I am not wary of reality, of which I know practically nothing, but I have suspicions concerning the image of reality brought to us by our senses, one which is incomplete and limited.... I cannot describe anything more clearly concerning reality than my own relation to reality. And the latter always has to do with the blurred, with insecurity, inconsistency, fragmentariness and who knows what else.[31]

The impreciseness of the contours, however, plays a more precise role than that of a generalized metaphor, and once again in double fashion. The objectivity of the photograph, its quality as a ressembling sign, a "pure image," is tied to its own disappearance as an object to the benefit of what it refers to. The blurriness which affects the image, and which makes it a "bad icon," is first of all a reminder of its existence as an object, an existence the affirmation of which is inversely proportional to its ability to resemble and document.[32]

[30] "On one hand, the photo is already a little painting, while still not being one completely. This is an irritating characteristic, and makes you want to transform it definitively into a painting. On the other hand, the photograph possesses specific qualities which get away if one paints directly from nature." Quoted in Leeber, *op. cit.*, p. 15.

[31] In Schön, *Gerhard Richter*, Venice Biennale, *op. cit.*, p. 24.

[32] "To what extent is your photographic painting objective, in the sense of documentary description?" "Not at all. First of all, only photographs can be objective, for they are linked to an object without being objects themselves. In spite of everything, I can see them as an objects as well, and even better, make them into objects, by painting ..../...

Furthermore, the images produced by Richter are not photographs but paintings, that is, objects that have come to be dispossessed by photography of the ambition they once had to document the real. Nor can they be, as paintings, blurred:

> The paintings... are never blurred. What we think is indistinct is in fact inexactness, and that means being different when compared to the subject painted. But since paintings are not meant to be compared to reality, they cannot be indistinct or inexact or different (different from what?). How can the color on a canvas not be clear, for instance?[33]

If the viewer's first reaction before a photo-picture by Richter is to come closer, to adjust his distance to the picture in order to dissipate the blurriness and "get a better look," the result of this procedure is the progressive disaggregation of the already defective information offered by the image to the point of potential "catastrophe," the complete disappearance of iconic resemblance.[34] The latter gives way to the reality of the painting and to another mode of looking, disabused, in every sense of the word. This is one way to explain a statement by the painter:

> I never found anything missing in a blurry painting. On the contrary, one sees much more in it than in a sharp image. A landscape painted with exactitude requires you to see a given number of trees sharply differentiated, while in a blurry painting you can perceive any number of trees you wish.[35]

If one can see more in a blurry landscape than in a landscape painted "with exactitude," it is obviously not in the sense of documentary visual information, but rather in the sense that it becomes necessary for the viewer to decide what is indeterminate in the painting, and that in looking the viewer stop counting

---

.../... them, for example. Afterwards, they can no longer be, nor are they supposed to be, objective. Nor should they document anything, whether a reality or a way of seeing (*Anschaung*). They are reality and a way of seeing, that is, an object, themselves, and cannot be documented." *Ibid.*

[33] *Ibid.*

[34] On the "catastrophic" quality of Richter's paintings, see Jean-Pierre Criqui, "Three Impromptus on the Art of Gerhard Richter," *Parkett*, # 35 (1993), pp. 38-43.

[35] Lebeer, *op. cit.*, p. 15.

documentable objects to ask the necessary questions, about what he or she is seeing and about the inherent desire to see.

Landscape, the Task Proper to Painting

That the example cited here by Richter happens to be landscape owes nothing to chance. In fact, the problematics at work in the execution of photographs in paintings has its historical origin in the rise, around 1800, of the *landscape*, not only as a genre equal or superior in dignity to history painting, which until then had occupied the summit of the pictorial hierarchy,[36] but as the *task proper to painting* and as its future.

The clearest expression of this new situation and of the meaning attributed to it is to be found in a letter from the painter Philipp Otto Runge dated 1802:

> For us something is in the process of passing away; we are at the very limits of the religions derived from Catholicism; abstractions are perishing; everything is airier and lighter than before; *everything aspires to the landscape*; something determined is being sought in this indeterminacy, but knows not where to begin; wrongly, we return to history and find ourselves in a fog.[37]

[36] See. for example Félibien: "Thus, he who makes landscapes perfectly is superior to another who does only fruits, flowers or shells... And since the figure of man is the most perfect handiwork of God on earth, it is also certain that he who makes himself the imitator of God by painting human figures is much more excellent than all the others... Nonetheless a Painter who does only portraits has not yet attained that high perfection of the Art & may not claim to the honor received by the most learned. For this one must pass from one figure to the representation of several together. One must treat of history & fable; one must represent great deeds as do the Historians, or pleasing subjects, as do the Poets. And climbing even higher, one must, by allegorical compositions, learn how to cover with the veil of fable the virtues of great men and the loftiest of mysteries." *Conférences de l'Académie royale de Peinture et de Sculpture pendant l'année 1667*, quoted by Jean-Claude Lebensztejn, *L'art de la tâche* (Montélimar, 1990), p. 263.

[37] Philipp Otto Runge, letter to Daniel Runge, February 1802; *Hinterlassene Schriften* (Gottingen, 1965 [Hamburg, 1840–1]), quoted in Jean-Claude Lebensztejn, *op. cit.*, pp. 267–68.

The painter and naturalist Carl Gustav Carus, student of Caspar David Friedrich, takes these declarations even further by speaking of landscape as "an art which truly characterizes modern times, which is further than one thinks from reaching its end, and will see its apogee only when most of the other arts come more to resemble the opposing faces of Janus, or come to rest, a sign of better days, on the tombs of the past."[38]

This *aspiration to landscape,* which Runge and Carus define as the aspiration to a truly modern art, appears against the background of the crisis of "abstractions," that is, of conventional symbolic modes in painting, itself occurring against the background of a spiritual and religious crisis of vast proportions. Against allegorical and historical modes, landscape offers the model of a painting where it is *the picture as a whole* and not one or another of its objects or figures which becomes the bearer of a meaning the determination of which also takes new pathways. This dislocation of the hierarchy of elements presented in the picture is first of all that of their syntax, and is the fruit of a new type of exercise of looking, in which the hand undergoes a profound devaluation. Commenting the landscapes of Le Lorrain, along with van Ruysdael one of the two *"founders of the art of landscapes,"* Carus observes that from the point of view of the "treatment of certain objects," the picture

> appears so strangely lackluster, one could almost say clumsy, that one thinks one is seeing a child's drawing. The clouds in both paintings have bizarre shapes in their details, heavy and almost unpleasant, and his painting of the sea seems the laborious result of an infinity of little lines. And yet — when you once again contemplate the whole of it — what serene vision, what intimate sensation of the beauty of nature are not spread out there?! The most subtle aromas join the

[38] Carl Gustav Carus, *Neuf lettres sur la peinture de paysage* [*Nine Letters on Landscape Painting*] (1831), in Caspar David Friedrich–Carl Gustav Carus, *De la peinture de paysage* (Paris, 1988), p. 63.

mountains to the forests, the calm undulation of the sea is portrayed with the greatest splendor, and the clouds, free and light, float over the warmed layers of air. One clearly senses that if these images have come to be fixed on canvas, it is because they presented themselves in this way and no other, with total clarity and lightness, to the eyes of the soul, whatever, in the end, may have been the clumsiness of the hand.[39]

If the very same forms here appear in turn, "heavy and un-pleasant" then "free and light," first a "laborious result" then rendered with "the greatest splendor," and always the effect of the same "clumsiness of hand," it is because of a change in the way one sees. If one ceases to be interested in isolated propositions and how they are rendered pictorially, one then begins to perceive, in an undifferentiated but coherent manner, the entire surface of the canvas, conceived as the most faithful transcription possible onto canvas of a prior "vision," the task of this trancription being to bring this vision into view without modifying it. The splendor of the landscape is entirely an effect of this new freshness of the gaze, with the role of the hand much reduced, bringing the image beyond the materiality of the picture. Carus stigmatizes Lorrain's "childish" technique not for its lack of pictoriality, but because it is stuck in a way of working paint that should be minimized, even entirely done away with, in favor of a transparency of vision whose realization ought to be simply a fixing. But Lorrain's manner goes in the other direction, too, in so far as it forgets the hand and guarantees the authenticity of the image, conceived as a purely interior vision.

Thus in the end Carus is able to proclaim, "If there is one place where we do not have to fear that one style will bring about a uniformity in works of art, that privileged place is landscape

---

[39] *Ibid.*, p. 98.

painting."[40] As a law for the latter, he proposes,

> the idea that there can only be one pure style and one truly proper treatment, the idea that in this guise individuality must fuse with the work, and that forgetting the hand in favor of the mind and spirit provides real proof of the excellence of the artwork.[41]

A unique way, once divested of its pictoriality, to bring into view the diverse and indifferentiated infinity of the objects of nature, landscape painting was already a way of beginning to work out the photographic gaze. It was even more so by the "airy and light" character, according to Runge, of its mode of signifying, at least in this new form of it, stripped of the last remaining finery which bound it to the history painting from which it had progressively disengaged itself: the tiny archaizing human figures which parsimoniously populated the paintings of Poussin or Lorrain, bringing to life the bits of nature presented to the eye and integrating them into history or fable.[42]

The best witness to this "airy and light" character is the painting of Caspar David Friedrich, which on its own completed the revolution prefigured by Runge. Ludwig Tieck, recalling a conversation with Novalis on the subject of painting, observed that the latter's views seemed to him at the time barely intelligible, but that "later" Friedrich, through the poetic richness of his character alone, was able to give these ideas "a totally realistic tenor." It was thus Friedrich who first gave a determinateness in visual form to ideas seeking expression in the indeterminateness of the landscape.[43]

---

[40] *Ibid.*, p. 87.

[41] *Ibid.*, p. 84. See. further: "One thing is absolutely certain: the highest and most excellent works of pure beauty will always have the greatest similarity, while the individuality of the artist, by putting itself in the foreground, moves the work away from the ideal." *Ibid.*, p. 86.

[42] If the Romantic landscape is not necessarily devoid of human presence, it plays an entirely different role there, as we shall see below.

[43] Rather than applying *a posteriori* to the domain of the image previously established formulations expressed in words. I have taken the reference to Tieck from Joseph Leo Koerner, and follow him in the conclusions he draws, especially in "Romanticism," chapter 3 of his *Caspar David Friedrich and the Subject of Landscape* (London, 1990), pp. 23–24.

The Landscape According to Friedrich

The first of Friedrich's great works, *The Crucifix on the Mountain* (or *The Tetschen Altarpiece*) provides one instance of this passage to new ideas. Theoretically destined to adorn the altar of a private chapel, the painting represents a fragment of a mountain landscape, a large rock surrounded by pines, at the summit of which rises a great cross, seen in three-quarter view from the rear in a dusky sky streaked by the rays of the setting sun. The work had great symbolic value for Friedrich, as he explained in a detailed interpretation in one of his letters,[44] but it was only the frame made for it that explicitly declared his objectives, directing the mind of the viewer to the search for symbols.[45] The image presented in the painting is a *view whose allegorical reading is entirely optional*: the crucifix has the same status as the pines (and in this case even to the point of being the same size), the rock and the rays of the sun. It is just as open to being given a symbolic meaning, as the other objects, within the framework of an overall meaning brought to the image by the gaze. As Friedrich said in a letter to the artist Louise Seidler where he briefly describes another of his paintings, *The Crucifix on the Shore of the Baltic*:

[44] "*Interpretation of the painting.* Jesus Christ, nailed to the wood of the cross, turns toward the setting sun, an image of the Eternal Father who gives life to everything. With the teachings of Jesus an old world passes away, a time when God the Father manifests Himself on earth without an intermediary. This sun has set, and the earth can no longer catch its dying light. It is then that the figure of the Savior, made of the noblest and purest metal, resplendent on the cross, made golden by the setting sun, is reflected with a soft glow here on earth. The cross rises from the rock, as unassailable as our faith in Jesus Christ. Still green, the pines, resistant to time, ring the rock like the hopes mankind puts in Him, the Crucified One." Caspar David Friedrich, letter to Friedrich August Schulz, in Friedrich–Carus, *op. cit.*, p. 151.

[45] "On the sides, the frame is composed of two gothic columns. Palms rise from these columns forming an arch above the painting. In the palms are five angel's heads in adoration looking at the cross below. Above the central angel's head the pure silver rays of the Evening Star. Below, in an oblong panel, the all-seeing eye of God set in the sacred triangle, surrounded by rays. Ears of corn and vines, symbols of the body and blood of the One hanging on the cross." *Ibid.*

The picture destined for your friend is already sketched out, but you will see in it neither church nor plant, not even a blade of grass. On the barren, rocky seashore rises tall the cross — *for those who see, a consolation; for those who do not, a cross.*[46]

One could not any more clearly affirm that it is the way the picture is viewed that brings the image to the symbol or not, a symbolism whose determination constitutes the impossible task assigned to the viewer by the picture.[47]

Replacing a traditional crucifixion with a landscape that included a crucifixion was potentially scandalous, as was noted by von Ramdohr, one of the first critics of the painting. He rebuked Friedrich for having "hoisted a landscape onto the altar," provoking a "pathological commotion" in the viewer.[48] Hoisting the landscape onto the altar was in effect proclaiming the end of traditional allegorical modes, relegated here to the frame and soon to be entirely abandoned, as well as at the same time declaring the quasi-religious value the landscape acquires as a *pure appearance of the real,* an undifferentiated one where crucifix, trees, mountain, sky and sun exist and signify on one and the same level; that of the *image.* This implies first of all the dissemination of the sacred into the totality of the real, whatever the necessarily fragmentary scene from it the artist chooses to present.[49] Furthermore, it becomes necessary, this time on the level of execution, to bring together this dispersion within a perfectly even and homogeneous facture:

Nothing is secondary in a painting; everything is absolutely necessary to the whole. Consequently, nothing should be neglected. If an artist

---

[46] *Ibid.*, p. 158 (emphasis mine).

[47] See. the complaints of the critic for the *Blätter für literarische Unterhaltung* in 1826: "... In truth one should call [Friedrich's] sketches artist's hieroglyphs or charades; everyone may interpret them according to their own mind, and they seize the imagination much more than they satisfy the eye." Quoted in *Tout l'œuvre peint de Caspar David Friedrich*, (Paris, 1976), p. 11.

[48] Friedrich–Carus, *op. cit.*, p. 46, note 79.

[49] We should remember Friedrich's comment before his painting *The Swan in the Rushes*, reported by the painter Peter Cornelius: "The divine is everywhere, even in a grain of sand. Here, for example, it is in the rushes." *Ibid.*, p. 64, note 1.

can only bring out the major portion of his painting by neglecting the treatment of the other parts, the secondary ones, his work risks turning out quite badly.[50]

This last point might make Friedrich appear closer to his fellow landscape artists were it not for the hallucinatory precision of his hand, applied in this case to scenes from which the traditionally picturesque elements have first been banished.[51] From this point of view, *The Monk on the Seashore* [ill. 29], the second of Friedrich's great works after *The Tetschen Altarpiece*, in its explicit radicality enlightens us as to the painter's intentions, judging from the apprehensiveness of which it became the object among his immediate contemporaries.[52]

The first of the reactions to the painting that has come down to us is that of Marie-Hélène von Kügelgen, the wife of a painter friend of Friedrich's. Back from a visit to his studio, where she had seen the painting as it was being worked on, she began describing it to a woman friend by declaring that it "did not at all speak to her soul." Once she had briefly described the components of the image — "an immense sky, infinite, below it a choppy sea and in the foreground a strip of white sand on which a hermit slowly walked" — she continued her description with a litany-like enumeration of what was not in the painting, but should have been there in order for the soul to find "consolation and pleasure." "Not the smallest skiff, not the slightest boat, not even any marine

[50] *Ibid.*, pp. 155–56.

[51] See. I. Schopenhauer's remarks in the *Journal des Luxus und der Moden* (1810): "Friedrich's work is noticeably different from that of other landscape artists, above all in the choice of subjects. Air, which he treats with the hand of a true master, takes up more than half the space in most of his paintings, and the middle- and backgrounds are often missing, as he chooses subjects which do not require their being represented. He delights in painting unlimited stretches. Faithful to the true in the most infinitesimal detail, he also reaches a very high level of perfection in his art, whether it is oil painting or sepia drawing." Quoted in *Tout l'œuvre peint de Caspar David Friedrich, op. cit.*, p. 12.

[52] In the catalogue for the exhibition at the Academy in which it was exhibited for the first time, it was mentioned, with its counterpart *The Abbey in the Woods*, under the generic title of *landscape*.

life, and in the sand not the slightest blade of grass."[53] Here Friedrich's painting seems to confront the viewer not with the image presented, but with images whose absence seems to haunt him or her as she looks at the painting.[54]

The same feeling of absence, here objectified in the form of representations missing from the painting, also structures the entire wonderful account of the painting composed unwittingly by Arnim, Brentano and Kleist at the first exhibition of the painting in Berlin:[55]

> How marvelous it is to contemplate this infinite desert of water from the beaches of the north in perfect solitude and under a gray sky. But it is because one has been there and back that the desire to return there seizes us, one impossible to satisfy in the moment, although it remains so vital to life. Yet it is there that one senses the living vibration, in the lapping of the waves, the whispering of the wind, the crashing of the surf, the lonesome cries of the birds. This was the charge formulated by my heart to the painting, the bar, so to speak, that nature arouses in us. But this was impossible in the

[53] The entire description is as follows: "I saw a rather large oil painting which speaks to my soul not at all: an immense sky, infinite, below it a choppy sea and in the foreground a strip of white sand on which a hermit slowly walked. The sky was pure and calm [an element later modified by the painter]; there was no tempest, no sun, no storm. A storm would have been a relief and a pleasure for me, for one would at least have had a feeling of life and movement. On this vast stretch of sea one sees not the smallest skiff, not the slightest boat, nor even any marine life, and in the sand not the slightest blade of grass. Only a few gulls sailing by here and there, making the loneliness even more lonely and sinister." Quoted in Helmut Borsch-Supan, *Caspar David Friedrich* (Paris, 1989), p. 82. Note the similarity in approach to Friedrich's description of the *Crucifix on the Shore of the Baltic*; there, too, the painter begins by listing what is not in the painting. See above, p. 73.

[54] Today, thanks to infrared photographs of the painting we know that Friedrich had initially planned two ships in distress for his composition. The composition of the work is thus itself caught up in a process of erasure of determinant elements.

[55] The text is in fact Kleist's revision of the account by Clemens Brentano in collaboration with Achim von Arnim. By cutting from the text a series of short dialogues by visitors rather hostile to the painting and adding his own reaction, Kleist denatured the original sense of the text and "made a critical account into an enthusiastic effusion," as Henri Koerner writes. *Tout l'œuvre peint de Caspar David Friedrich, op. cit.*, p. 6). The strange leaps and staggers in the thinking are doubtless an effect of this writing by three hands.

presence of the painting, for what I ought to have found in the image itself I would discover only between the painting and myself, namely a charge that my heart addressed to the image, a claim which was barred by it. Thus I myself became the friar, and the image became the dune, but where I strove to look with all my heart, the sea persistently failed me. There can be nothing sadder or more uncomfortable in this world — the only spark of life in a vast kingdom of death, the solitary center of a solitary circle. The painting is there with its two or three mysterious objects, like an apocalypse reflecting Young's night thoughts. In its uniformity and absence of shore it has but the frame for a foreground, and when one looks at it, one has the feeling one's eyelids have been cut off.[56]

This admirable text, although primarily a quite precise description of the experience induced by contemplating the painting, also describes in a more general way the efficacy of the landscape as conceived by Friedrich. The first moment is the feeling evoked in the viewer by the image represented, the infinity of sky and sea seen from the strand The immediate effect of the painting is to direct the viewer to the objects it represents, but in the form of the trace left by a past experience. This is affirmed by the figure of the contemplating monk, whose presence implies that the scene has already been seen, and resituates the spectator's view as a doubling of the experience, one lagging behind the first, the latter also portrayed but indirectly.

This first moment of experience, where the painting seems to fade into the memory it represents, is immediately nullified, both by the awareness that the desire to go back is impossible to satisfy in the present, and by the indeterminate state into which the painting plunges us. When Kleist writes, "Yet it is there that one senses the living vibration, in the lapping of the waves, the whispering of the wind," and so on, the synesthetic *there* of which he

[56] Heinrich von Kleist, "Impressions of Friedrich's Seascapes," *Berliner Abendblatter*, quoted in Borsch-Supan, *op. cit.*, p. 82–3.

speaks to his readers cannot be confused with the pictorial image, any more than it is identical to the original experience of which it strives to be the trace.

The viewer's demand that from the picture he be able to return to the wonder of past experiences of contemplating nature is also a demand that the work provide *here and now* the feelings that nature had previously refused to confirm. When the heart of the viewer addresses this demand to the picture, it is not only because he finds himself far removed from the seashore, but because even when he was there, nature had remained mute to his demand. Thus the picture, far from fulfilling the demand with its presence, only dismisses it and reiterates the non-receivability of the charge. The image has no objective externals. It does not refer to the objects it represents, but to the space in between which separates it from the viewer, in the form of the demand the latter addresses to it and the dismissal it opposes to this claim.[57] Whence "the feeling one's eyelids have been cut off," that is, of having to keep on looking, even where the visible is abolished as representation, even where the sea "fails" us and the shore becomes absence.

This dialectic of the gaze — aspiring to see the picture, but forced to continue looking at something that sleeps away — is induced by the very composition of the image: the ends of the white sandy beach form a flattened triangle with the base of the painting, and the legs from the apex serve as diagonals of perspective They draw the eye deep in, to the incongruous silhouette of the standing monk. Symmetrically, an "airy and light" triangle is formed between the upper edge of the painting and the moon, half-hidden in the clouds, which is directly above the figure of the

[57] This is the relationship portrayed, among others in the painting, by the figure of the monk. His verticality, and his disproportion to the other elements portrayed, make him seem somewhat removed with respect to the rest of the scene, which reiterates within the painting the relationship of the viewer to it. This is also what comes through from setting off the sightlines of the monk and the viewer. If one remains in one's place before the painting, one does not see what the monk does; if one identifies with him, one no longer sees the painting.

monk. Between the two peaks — moon and monk — which mark the distances, lies a space which refuses all depth, even though it portrays the horizon, and which leads us back to the two-dimensionality of the pictorial plane. What the monk is looking at reveals nothing except the flat opacity of the paint and the dismissal of the aspiration of the gaze to representation.[58]

The structure of the image as described here — the accession of the viewer to the picture is marked by various leads into the picture for the gaze, its sudden blockage and the maintenance of this tension by the coexistence of opposites — can be found in most of Friedrich's paintings, although the manner in which it is executed varies. One of these takes on a very particular cast: the invention of the landscape invaded by mist, or by images of fog. One small painting, traditionally entitled *Fog*, which antedates the *Monk* by two years, provides the most radical example [ill. 28]. There is an extreme contrast between the bare and precise foreground formed by the strand, where the diagonal arrangement of the rocks outlines the beginnings of a perspective, and the opaque screen formed by the rest of the painting, where the sea and sky are identifiable as such only by the inscription of the very light silhouettes of a skiff and a boat on the verge of disappearing. The locus of what is happening here is that "in-between" which separates, on the one hand, a foreground where everything is precisely laid out but where nothing gives off Kügelgen's "feeling of life or movement," and, on the other a completely indeterminate background where representation risks obliteration. Friedrich used this formula on several occasions, in his *Boat on the Elbe* (ca. 1821), for example, or in *Mountain Landscape in the Early-Morning Mist* (1808), which uses banks of mists to present

---

[58] See. Joseph Leo Koerner, *op. cit.*, p. 119–21. This screen effect is if possible even more pronounced the thickness of the paint in that spot because of Friedrich's repainting, and which stands as a contradiction to the supposed diaphanousness of the sky.

a series of layered planes spatially indeterminate. Friedrich himself offered a theory for this use of the misty:

> When a landscape is covered in mist, it appears grander and more sublime. It strengthens the power of the imagination and arouses our expectation, just like a veiled woman. The eye and our fantasy are more readily attracted by nebulous distance than by what lies closer and more distinctly before us.[59]

To paint a landscape covered in mist is to declare the veil which affects the very act of looking, and to forbid the latter to obliterate itself in seeking to determine the object, in order to open it to the apprehension of the sublime through the powers of the imagination and the expectation of desire.[60]

Painting Like C. D. Today

Friedrich's observation on the benefits of the use of the veil as an imagining force in looking bring us back once again to the statements of Richter quoted above on the photographic "blurriness" of his landscapes. The coincidence is not accidental. Richter in effect claims for his photo-paintings the designation "Romantic," in two senses of the word. The first is the vague sense of the contemporary cliché which associates romanticism and beauty; there is also the other sense, that of an authentic historical relationship, one which is not obliterated by the cliché-like character of

[59] Quoted in Koerner, *op. cit.*, p. 181. One might compare Friedrich's phrase with Schelling's statement, "Landscape painting necessarily opens out onto empirical truth, but the best it can do is to use it again as a veil, in order to allow a higher order of truth to appear in it. *But only the veil is represented; the true objet, the idea, is devoid of any portrayal, and it is up to the observer to uncover it by stripping it of its vaporous and shapeless essence.*" "Le Monde des tableaux ['The World of Paintings']" in *Philosophie de l'Art. Textes esthétiques* (Paris, 1978), p. 95 (emphasis mine).

[60] See. Friedrich: "The painter should not only paint what he sees before him, but also what he sees in himself. But if he sees nothing in himself, he would be better off not painting what he sees before him, either." In Friedrich–Carus, *op. cit.*, p. 170. Friedrich goes on to say, "Otherwise paintings would resemble screens behind which one expects to find the sick, even the dead." Paintings with something behind them are bad paintings. In a good painting, something happens *between* the painting and the viewer.

the notion.[61] This relationship is based on the fact "the paintings from that time are now part of our sensibility. Otherwise we would no longer look at them. Romanticism is far from being liquidated. Just like fascism."[62]

As shown in a letter from the painter to Jean-Christophe Amman, this romanticism has a proper name:

> All my paintings are in fact *informel*... with the possible exception of the landscapes. A painting by Caspar David Friedrich is not something from the past; the only things from the past are certain of the circumstances which brought about its appearing, that is, certain ideologies. That is why one can paint like C. D. "today."[63]

"Painting like C. D." is a possibility which takes on several meanings. In the first place, it marks the conscious takeover by Richter of themes established by Friedrich, from the point of view both of subject-matter as well as its composition. Thus, Richter's *Maritime (Wave)* [ill. 6] matches Friedrich's *Sun Rising Over the Sea*, not only because their manifest subject-matter — the horizon between sea and sky, a wave like a bead on the surface of the sea — is identical, but because of the radical separation of planes common to both works, a separation accentuated by Richter, who used composite photographs to make this series of works. The respective planes of sky and sea come from different photographic prints, cut along the line of the horizon and glued together.[64]

---

[61] "There is with me an authentic reference to Romanticism which differentiates me from the hyperrealists who represent the whole world of the present day, with its cars, superhighways, etc." Quoted in Lebeer, *op. cit.*, p. 16.

[62] *Ibid.* The relevance of the the Romantic past is far from true of the whole history of art. Speaking of Titian's *Annunciation*, which was the starting point of a cycle of paintings in 1979, Richter realized that, though starting from the desire to make a copy, he could only manage to "decompose everything, and thus show that it could no longer be done." *It*, namely both Titian's painting and its copy. Thus there exist historical moments in the pictorial tradition which, unlike Romanticism, are no longer accessible, both because of the values they convey and because of the "allegorical" means with which they are made manifest. See. Storsve, *op. cit.*, p. 16.

[63] Gerhard Richter, letter to Jean-Christophe Ammann (February 24, 1973), quoted in *Gerhard Richter* (Tate Gallery), *op. cit.*, p. 111.

[64] See. the plate *Seestücke* [*Seapieces*] in *Atlas* (1969). Here, too, Richter goes back to archaic practices in landscape photography, now taken out of their original context.

One can also compare Richter's *Clouds (Atmosphere)* or the *Great Landscape in Teyde* (1971) [ill. 9] to Friedrich's *Evening* (1824), or *The Monk on the Seashore* [ill. 29], the *Landscape with Small Bridge* [ill. 5] and the *Landscape near Hubbelrath* (1969) to the *Monk*. There, as in Friedrich's painting, a primary plane, reduced to a narrow strip but crossed with diagonals, is opposed to the vast opaque plane of the sky. In the same way, the famous *Rücken-figuren*, those figures seen from the back which constitute one of Friedrich's favorite ways to draw in the viewer,[65] make their appearance in Richter's *Königstein* (1987) [ill. 18], a composition extra-ordinarily close in spirit to *Monk on the Seashore* in the brutal rupture it establishes between the principal planes of the painting, as well as in the limit set for the advancing figures looking ahead in the painting and the indeterminateness of the object of their gaze.[66]

"Painting like C. D." today does not simply mean taking over themes from which in other respects Richter has distanced himself. With the exception doubtless of *Königstein*, Richter's production of landscapes during the' 80s ceased to make references to Friedrich in such a direct manner. Witness paintings like *Bushes* (1987) [ill. 17] or *Barn* (1984) [ill. 16], which though still attached to a pictorial problematics of the landscape that is pre-Impressionist, recall much more than Friedrich's do the compositions of Constable or the early Corot.

What remains, then, of the determinations put into operation in Friedrich's landscape is an image structure conceived as a capture of the gaze which almost immediately shifts into an impossibility of bringing clearly into view the object represented. In Friedrich's paintings this shift was effected either by the opaque screen formed by the advance of mist or fog, and their opposition

---

[65] See. for example *Two Men Contemplating the Moon* (ca. 1817).
[66] These analogies of theme are restricted to relationships between paintings. Thus, the series of photos taken by Richter during a trip to Greenland and later published as a book recalls very precisely Friedrich's *Sea of Ice* (1823–4), a painting which itself owes much illustrations which appeared in the press and to the panorama of the polar regions exhibited in Dresden in 1822.

to any obssessive sharpness of contour in nearby objects, or else by the indeterminacy of the spatial planes in relation to one another, generally brought about by the suppression or exacerbation of the usual perspectival reference points.[67] In Richter's work the shift in looking no longer operates the way it did for Friedrich, within the represented image, but, because of the pictorial nature of photographic "blur," even prior to it.[68] In addition, this structure is no longer exclusively limited to the landscapes, but is extended to all of the photo-paintings. Their photographic "look" refers to a "This was seen," to the experience of a "looking" prior to that of the viewer before the painting. In turn the photographic "blur," affecting the representation with its indeterminacy, simultaneously makes looking indeterminate, and renders it powerless to find a stable point from which to look. Finally, this "blur" is itself rendered indeterminate by its *painted* facture.

One could, paraphrasing Runge, affirm that it is the photo-paintings as a whole which "aspire to the landscape," that is, to the problematics of the image established by Friedrich. No longer deployed within the *genre* of landscape, it goes into effect ahead of the content of the representation, in the apparatus of the fabrication of the image. In this sense, *Record Player* (1988) [ill. 20], a painting from the *October 18, 1977* cycle (devoted to the controversial deaths of members of the Red Army Faction), aspires to landscape no less

---

[67] Thus the Duke of Saxony-Gotha-Altenburg, rather incisively, criticized the painter's work for presenting "frontal planes like mosaics and... backgrounds like geographic maps." See Borsch-Supan, *op. cit.*, p. 90.

[68] One can again see the effect of the photographic trauma in this transformation. In Friedrich's painting, the reality effect comes from the extreme precision devoted to the rendering of objects and their contours, and it is on the basis of this reality effect that the strategies to limit looking are put into operation. For Richter, once photography took over the reality effect of the image, and as a result relieved painting of it, the pictorial manifestation of the blur no longer had to be defined in contrast to the zones—often, although not always the foregrounds—which for Friedrich assured this effect. It was the surface of the painting as a whole which, by becoming "blurred," functioned as a limit to looking. Furthermore, while for Friedrich the model for the reality effect was still internal to the painting, for Richter it has moved to the outside: the photographic look, to the reproduction of which the imitative virtuosity of the painter is now restricted.

than *Rhine Landscape* or *Bushes* do, and one could define the photo-paintings in their entirety as the continuation of landscape by other means.

This functional equivalence leads one, however, to ask two questions. First of all, within what one might call the generalized "landscaping" of painting, what role does the *theme* of the landscape play? What continues to differentiate *Bushes* and *Barn* from *Record Player*? And second, what position do these same landscapes occupy with respect to the abstract paintings whose production they punctuate at regular intervals?

The Lie of the Landscape

One may have already concluded from the foregoing analyses that the *theme* of landscape has a primary function as a signal: the formal kinship of certain paintings with those of Friedrich declares the historical origin of the problematics put into place with the photo-paintings. This kinship clarifies the ins and outs of the matter, but its efficacy goes beyond this aspect of it alone.

The "romanticism" of the landscapes is in fact also valid on the level of the cliché, still current, but somewhat *kitschig*, to use the painter's expression, which makes the landscape into an ideal of beauty. Richter says of his landscapes from the end of the 60s that they are an attempt to "see to what extent we can still use beauty today. If it is still conceivable today." This attempt resulted in the deadpan conclusion that "it still has just as much impact."[69] Whereas the first photo-paintings explorent a zone of "esthetic anesthesia," in the Duchampian sense, the landscapes ask the question of "using beauty," and primarily of its role as a decoy. If with their content

---

[69] "For two years you painted clouds, landscapes and lakes of such ideal beauty that they practically became stereotypes of it. Why did you again slide back into cliché there?" "I wanted to see to what extent we can still use beauty today. If it is still conceivable today." "And what conclusion did you come to?" "That it still has just as much impact." In *Lebeer, op. cit.*, p. 15.

they display the recurring power and contemporary efficacy of the romantic cliché, at the same time they signify its projective power through the traps of indeterminateness it lays for looking.

In 1986, Richter wrote in his *Journal*:

My landscapes are not only beautiful or nostalgic, romantic or classical in appearance, presenting the appearances of lost paradises. They are above all "liars"... and by liars I mean the transfigured quality of the way we think about nature. Nature in all its forms is constantly against us, because it knows no meaning, pity nor compassion, because it knows nothing, has absolutely no mind or spirit, is the complete opposite of us and absolutely inhuman.

Any beauty we see in the landscape, any enchanting color, peacable mood, soft delineation, grand spaces, or whatever, is our own projection, one we can also interrupt so as to see only the terrifying ugliness and hideousness.[70]

What is staged in the landscapes is, once again, not the illusory nature of representation, but the projective quality of the idea of Nature embodied in the landscape.[71] By fabricating a beauty whose structure continually brings into play the aporias of the gaze that falls upon it, Richter displays this beauty *with* its projective character, a projective character which, though revealed, does not nullify the efficacy of the beautiful.

This aspect distinguishes Richter's landscapes from those of Friedrich, of which they appear to be a critique. When Friedrich set up barriers to the gaze which prevented one from being engulfed, it was in order to render the divinity of Nature more present to the senses. For Richter, unlike Kant, the veil which affects representation is not that of Isis.[72] It belongs to the very structure of the human gaze and makes the relationship between reality and image

[70] Quoted in *Gerhard Richter*, Tate Gallery, *op. cit.*, p. 117.

[71] "The illusion, as an optical ruse, does not figure among the means I employ, and my paintings are not illusionist, either." Quoted in Schön, *Gerhard Richter*, Venice Biennale, *op. cit.*, p. 23.

[72] "For me, what is missing is the spiritual foundation underlying Romantic painting We have lost the feeling of the ubiquity of God in Nature. For us everything is empty. And yet the paintings are still there, and they speak to us. We continue to love them, to use them and to need them." Quoted in *Lebeer, op. cit.*, p. 16. If.../

undecidable. All we see is image, but we do not know of what. Furthermore, images have a fundamentally indexical structure: they *indicate* the real, without letting us know anything more about it than the property of being real, without giving us an image, or even an idea, of it.

At this point it becomes necessary to deal with a second question: that of the relationship between the landscapes and the abstract paintings, of which they have been, since the 70s, a lesser counterpart. If the function of the landscapes is to have us experience natural beauty, its projective character, and the mendacious character of the tranfiguration worked on Nature, the *abstract paintings* in fact intimate the possibility of another relationship to Nature.

Abstraction, nature, photography

Abstract paintings, writes Richter, are "fictional models," for they make our senses aware of a reality which we can neither see nor describe, but whose reality we can infer. It is this reality that we define in negative concepts — un-known, in-conceivable, in-finite — and for millennia we have described them with ersatz or replacement images like the sky, hell, the gods and demons.

With abstract painting we have created for ourselves a better possibility of approaching something that is non-visual and incomprehensible, because it depicts "nothing" directly, with all the means at the disposal of the art.[73]

We all know the cutting remark, quoted by Hazlitt with respects to certain paintings of Turner's: "Pictures of nothing, and very like." It could just as well be applied, without any of the

/... one was to associate Richter with one Enlightenment philosopher—perhaps a futile move—rather than Kant, it would be Hume, with his unstable dialectic between scepticism and hope, that comes to mind.

[73] From a text published on the occasion of Documenta 7, 1982, quoted in *Gerhard Richter*, Tate Gallery, *op. cit.*, p. 112–3.

negative connotations, to Richter's abstract paintings.[74] These, too, in fact, *represent nothing*, and show it better than paintings that propose symbolic or allegorical images, in that they abandon — at least up to a certain point, one which we shall attempt to determine below — the ambition of iconic resemblance, in order to concentrate on the indexical pole of the image.

The first abstract paintings used the technique of the photo-paintings: Richter painted on a canvas projected photographs of small abstract sketches.[75] Starting in 1980 he abandoned this procedure. Beginning with an often geometric and brightly colored initial composition, he now covers it in successive super-impositions of strata and streaks of paint until — the original composition having disappeared under these successive markings — "there was no longer anything I could do [to these paintings]; either they are way beyond me, or they have something I could no longer equal."[76] [ill. 23] The image he started with, composed and laden with everything a subjectivity in quest of a theme can put into it, is therefore destroyed as an image, in order to allow the gradual appearance of a variety of painting-events which, having been produced semi-mechanically, escape ordering and the hierarchy of subjectivity. The final image is the spatial record of this variety. From this point of view, the term *abstract painting* far from reflecting the process of producing the paintings, has, as do the landscapes, a "mendacious" character.[77]

[74] I owe this reference to the excellent discussion in Jean-Pierre Criqui, *op. cit.*, p. 41.

[75] "That's when I painted some very small, abstract works from photos and I didn't quite dare to consider them regular paintings. I looked at them as purely subjective. That is why I copied them, to objectify them." Interview with Dorothea Dietrich, *op. cit.*, p. 128. Here we can see the Romantic landscape painters' preoccupation with getting away from individual subjectivity in their painting style. See. Carus' observations on the "pure style," of landscape painting, with its tendency towards unity.

[76] Comments taken from Peter Sager, "Mit der Farbe denken," ["Thinking with Painting"], *Zeitmagazin*, # 49 (November 28, 1986), quoted by Roald Nasgaard in *Gerhard Richter: Bilder/Paintings 1962–1985, op. cit.*, p. 108.

[77] As Stephan Germer observes, The *Gestalt* of these paintings is not the result of a process of abstraction, that is, the reduction of a multiplicity of its basic elements, but results instead from a process of "concretization," "the course of which brings.../

Destroying the image as composition and direct subjective expression in order to replace it with a painting that is the physical trace of a process is to update *in painting* the initial assault of photography against painting. In this primary sense, the abstract paintings remain "photographic," and in the end it is to them that the remark of Richter's chosen to introduce this essay might best be applied, a remark which initially was aimed at the photo-paintings:

> I want to make a photograph. And if by photograph one means a piece of printed paper, then I make photographs by other means, and not images that have something of the photo about them.[78]

Photographs the paintings are in several other respects. As has been said, Richter's undertaking, although it plays on the opposition between abstraction and figurativeness, does not deal with the problem of representation and its illusions, but with the problem of what the image — *any image* — takes on. In this sense the painter may declare with no contradiction that on one hand illusion is not among the means he employs, and that his paintings are not illusionist, and on the other that every painting, including Malevich's *Black Square*, is illusionist.[79] In the former case it is a question of declaring illusion conceived as a simple "optical ruse" null and void, and in the latter of proclaiming that all painting is of necessity in a relationship with reality, a relationship that Richter

/... about the appearance of a variety of accidental elements." In Stefan Germer, "Retrospective Ahead," in *Gerhard Richter*, Tate Gallery, *op. cit.*, p. 30.

[78] Quoted in Schön, *Gerhard Richter*, Venice Biennale, *op. cit.*, p. 23. This remains true in spite of Richter's tendency to want to distance the abstract paintings from photography. See. the interview with Dorothea Dietrich, where Richter 'forgets' his use of photographs in the abstract paintings before 1980. In Dietrich, *op. cit.*, p. 128.

[79] "If you see nothing in Malevich's *Black Square*, then painting will only be a dumb black spot." *Ibid.*, p. 131. See also: "I am not ready to... accept any great difference between pure paintings [*Bildern*], which represent only themselves, and those that copy. For example, the paintings of Ryman, Palermo and Marden are also illusionist paintings. It may even happen that one is able to see color [*Farbe*, also "paint"], the pure material, only with a certain effort, for example if one sees it with the eye of a paint dealer..." Interview with Gislind Nbakowski, *Heute Kunst*, Milan, July/August 1974, quoted in *Gerhard Richter: Bilder/Paintings 1962–1985*, *op. cit.*, p. 58–9.

continues to think in practice, even in his "abstractions," in terms of an analogy with the photographic apparatus.

The quasi-photographic apparatus of the abstract paintings is obvious in the image-structure it promotes. Jean-Pierre Criqui recently observed the extent to which these paintings, unlike the tradition of abstract art and a part of the figurative art of the twentieth century, displayed a striking "abhorrence of the void"; they know neither "reserve" nor the use of the support as such.[80] This *horror vacui* can be explained, however, if one just considers them not as paintings, but as *images* in the quasi-photographic sense of the word. In a photo, the whole of the printed surface is a trace of real events, whatever their nature and heterogeneity; this includes all the mistakes and accidents possible during shooting or development. The abstract paintings work in the same way; they comprise a screen on which the entire group of procedures, whatever they may be, are inscribed there.[81] "I want the painting to be very heterogeneous," Richter has said. "Nevertheless everything should be from the same mold, as contradictory as that may sound."[82]

The quasi-photographic nature of the abstract paintings is also attested by the mode of *a posteriori* framing constituted by the

---

[80] Criqui, *op. cit.*, p. 42.

[81] This characteristic explains, it seems to me, Richter's otherwise strange remark to Irmeline Lebeer: "I don't know anything about space in painting." "Does it not interest you?" "It doesn't exist. It's a fake issue." In Lebeer, *op. cit.*, p. 15. The question of space ceases to be an issue in painting when the work, as an window open on the world, becomes the screen/veil onto which are imprinted events, whatever their pictorial mode of production, all belonging to the real. Here, too, the Romantic landscape was the historical locus of this transition. This is attested even by Friedrich's paintings of a figure at a window, apparently far removed from the new tasks of painting. By displacing the structure of the window of representation to the represented, the paintings also displace the sense and direction of the act of looking. The painting ceases being an immediate perception of what is being shown and takes on a story or history, one whose reconstitution becomes the infinite task of the viewer.

[82] Dietrich, *op. cit.*, p. 128. It should be noted that the only element of homogeneity in the paintings is defined here in terms of *imprinting*.

titles given to certain of them, names of places or persons, *always provided after the fact*, which give verbal form to the impressions the painting evokes in the artist, who is then but the first spectator of the work.[83] These *names* are not traditional descriptive titles, like those of the landscape. Like the *captions* of photographs once analysed by Benjamin, they are distinguished by their claim to orient in words the apprehension of a visually non-hierarchized image.[84]

Yet if, as a reaction to the photo-paintings, the mission of the abstract paintings is at least partially to leave behind the problems posed by iconic resemblance, the ties developed to the photographic lead them to encounter, *at the limit of the index*, so to speak, the very questions of iconic resemblance they were seemingly to have escaped. If Richter can title an abstract painting *Forest* [ill. 23] without being simply arbitrary, it is because the way it works as a surface for inscription allows painting-events to be imprinted on its surface in a way analogous to the photographic inscription of reality. But if some other abstract painting [ill. 25] still reminds us of nature, it is also because visually it resembles photos like those seen in *Atlas* [ill. 26, 27], as much in the form of the individuals elements shown there as because of the anarchy with which these same forms are deployed throughout the rectangular field.

Making abstract paintings the veil or screen where a series of events are set together invokes not only a quasi-photographic apparatus, but also the relationship between indexical and iconic poles to which it has given rise. This then exposes us to the return of resemblance from where it is now least expected — abstraction.

[83] For example, of *Forest* Richter said, "There seemed to me to be in these four paintings a Romantic mood which reminded me of a forest. In the blue there is a feeling of diffuse light, which is the reason I came upon this title." Quoted in in *Gerhard Richter* (Tate Gallery), *op. cit.*, p. 130.

[84] See Walter Benjamin, "The Work of Art in the Age of Mechanical Reproduction." One will also recall Duchamp's remarks concerning the function of the phrases chosen to go along with the readymades. They were "meant to carry the mind of the viewer off toward more verbal regions." In Duchamp, *op. cit.*, p. 191.

This is the paradox one faces in one of Richter's most recent series, the *Overpaintings* (*Übermalungen*, also called *Overpainted Photos* (*Übermalte Photographien*), small paintings done directly on photographic prints, or if you will, photographs smeared with painted traces [ill. 27]. In these works, whose modest size (standard-format color prints) emphasizes their fragmentary, undifferentiated character, the screen-like nature of the surface of the abstract paintings is disclosed with no trace of ambiguity. Symmetrically the iconic and analogical function of the painting events stands fully revealed: associated to the photographic ground, for the viewer the paint marks become so many possible iconic vectors. Finally, the distinction between photograph and painting, sometimes locally indecipherable at first glance, tends, as announced in the ambiguous and double title given the series, to its own obliteration.

That these works should have for the most part a photographic basis in views or fragments of landscapes should at this point no longer surprise us. More clearly than in any other series, the *Overpaintings* or *Overpainted Photographs* are in effect a practical demonstration that landscape is the obligatory passageway leading from painting to abstraction. This is the movement which occurred in the course of the nineteenth century, and whose heritage the Friedrichian descendance of certain Richter landscapes claims. But the *Overpaintings* also show, even to the "organic" ties they continue to maintain with photography, that at the limits of the process of abstraction, and contrary to what the great abstract painters may have expected, the image does not disappear in the maculation of the paint. If landscape was an obligatory stage in the search for abstraction — if within what can be pictured or "figured" it is what sends us back, with no allegorical recourse, to that which cannot, the "unfigurable" — it doubtless is also the figure which comes forth, refusing to cede to "nothing," when the gaze falls on the screen of the painting, even though one has ceased representing anything at all there, to instead distribute, semi-chaotically throughout it, traces of color.

Although it appears at first a limited and numerically minor genre in Richter's multifaceted work, the landscape continues to haunt the abstract paintings like a kind of limit. Landscape thus remains the nexus where the paradoxes attending on the relationship between photography, painting and the real all come together.

Photo Index

1: *Kahnfahrt* 1965/69 - 150 x 190 cm. Courtesy of Gerhard Richter.
2: *Onkel Rudi* (Uncle Rudi), 1965/*85* - 87 x 50 cm. Stredocescá Galerie, Prague. Ph: Hana Jarosová. Courtesy of Gerhard Richter.
3: *4 Glasscheiben* (4 Glass Panels), 1967/*160*. Glas und Eisen - 190 x 100 cm. Courtesy of Gerhard Richter.
4: *Stadtbild Paris*, 1968/*175* - 200 x 200 cm. Courtesy of Gerhard Richter.
5: *Landschaft mit kleiner Brücke* (Landscape with small Bridge), 1969/*227* - 120 x 150 cm. Courtesy of Gerhard Richter.
6: *Seestück (Welle)* (Maritime [Wave]), 1969/*234* - 200 x 200 cm. Courtesy of Gerhard Richter.
7: *Grau,* (Grey) 1970/*247 4* - 200 x 150 cm. Courtesy of Gerhard Richter.
8: *Wolke,* 1970/*270 3* - 200 x 300 cm. Courtesy of Gerhard Richter.
9: *Große Teyde-Landschaft (mit zwei Figuren)* (Great Landscape in Teyde), 1971/*284* - 200 x 300 cm. Courtesy of Gerhard Richter.
10: *Vermalung* (grau), 1972/*326 2* - 250 x 250 cm. Courtesy of Gerhard Richter.
11: *Verkündigung nach Titian* (Annunciation after Titian), 1973/*344 1* - 150 x 250 cm. Courtesy of Gerhard Richter.
12: *Rot-Blau-Gelb,* 1973/*335 2* - 200 x 200 cm. Courtesy of Gerhard Richter.
13: *256 Farben,* 1974/*352 3* - 222 x 414 cm. Courtesy of Gerhard Richter.
14: *Zwei Kerzen* (Two Candles), 1982/*499 1* - 150 x 100 cm. Courtesy of Gerhard Richter.
15: *Schädel* (Skull), 1983/*545 1* - 80 x 65 cm. Ph: George Meister. Courtesy of Gerhard Richter.

16: *Scheune* (Barn), 1984/*550 1* - 95 x 100 cm. Courtesy of Gerhard Richter.

17: *Buche* (Bushes), 1987/*637 1* - 82 x 112 cm. Courtesy of Gerhard Richter.

18: *Königstein*, 1987/*651 2* - 52 x 72 cm. Courtesy of Gerhard Richter.

19 (a, b, c): *Gegenüberstellung*, 1988/*671 1. 2. 3.* - 112 x 102 cm. Courtesy of Gerhard Richter.

20: *Plattenspieler* (Record Player), 1988/*672 2* - 62 x 83 cm. Courtesy of Gerhard Richter.

21: *Beerdigung* (October 18), 1988/*673* - 200 x 320 cm. Courtesy of Gerhard Richter.

22: *Abstraktes Bild*, 1990/*727* - 2teiling, 250 x 350 cm. Courtesy of Gerhard Richter.

23: *Wald*, 1990/*731 1* - 340 x 260 cm. Courtesy of Gerhard Richter.

24: *Spiegel* (grey), 1991/*735 2*, farbig beschichtetes Glas, framed 280 x 165 cm. Courtesy of Gerhard Richter.

25: *Abstraktes Bild*, 1992/*780 1* - 260 x 200 cm. Courtesy of Gerhard Richter.

26: *Meerbusch* - ATLAS p. 140 (upper half). Courtesy of Gerhard Richter.

27: *Übermalungen* - ATLAS p. 227 (upper half). Ph: George Meister. Courtesy of Gerhard Richter.

28: Caspar David Friedrich, *Brouillard*, 1807. Oil on Canvas 34,5 x 52 cm. Vienna Art Historical Museum. © D.R

29: Caspar David Friedrich, *The Monk Beside the Sea*, 1809-1810. Oil on Canvas 110 x 171,5 cm. Berlin, National Gallery (Romanticist Gallery). © D.R

◀ 1

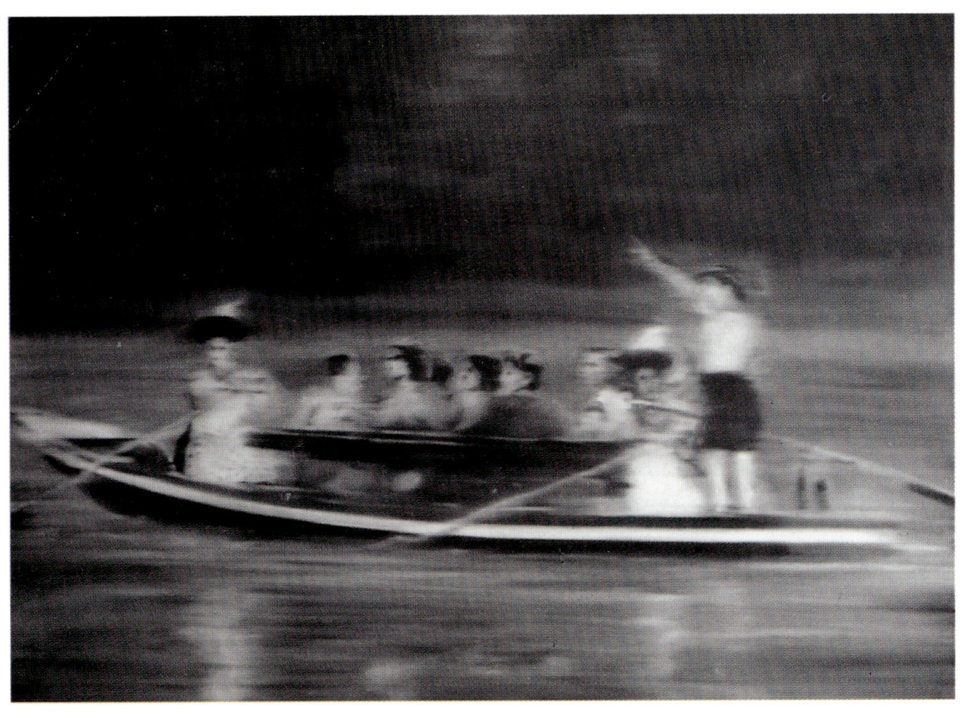

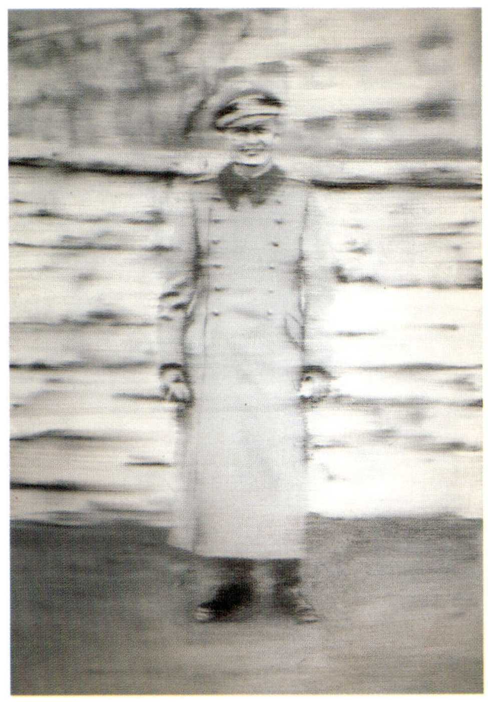

◀ 2

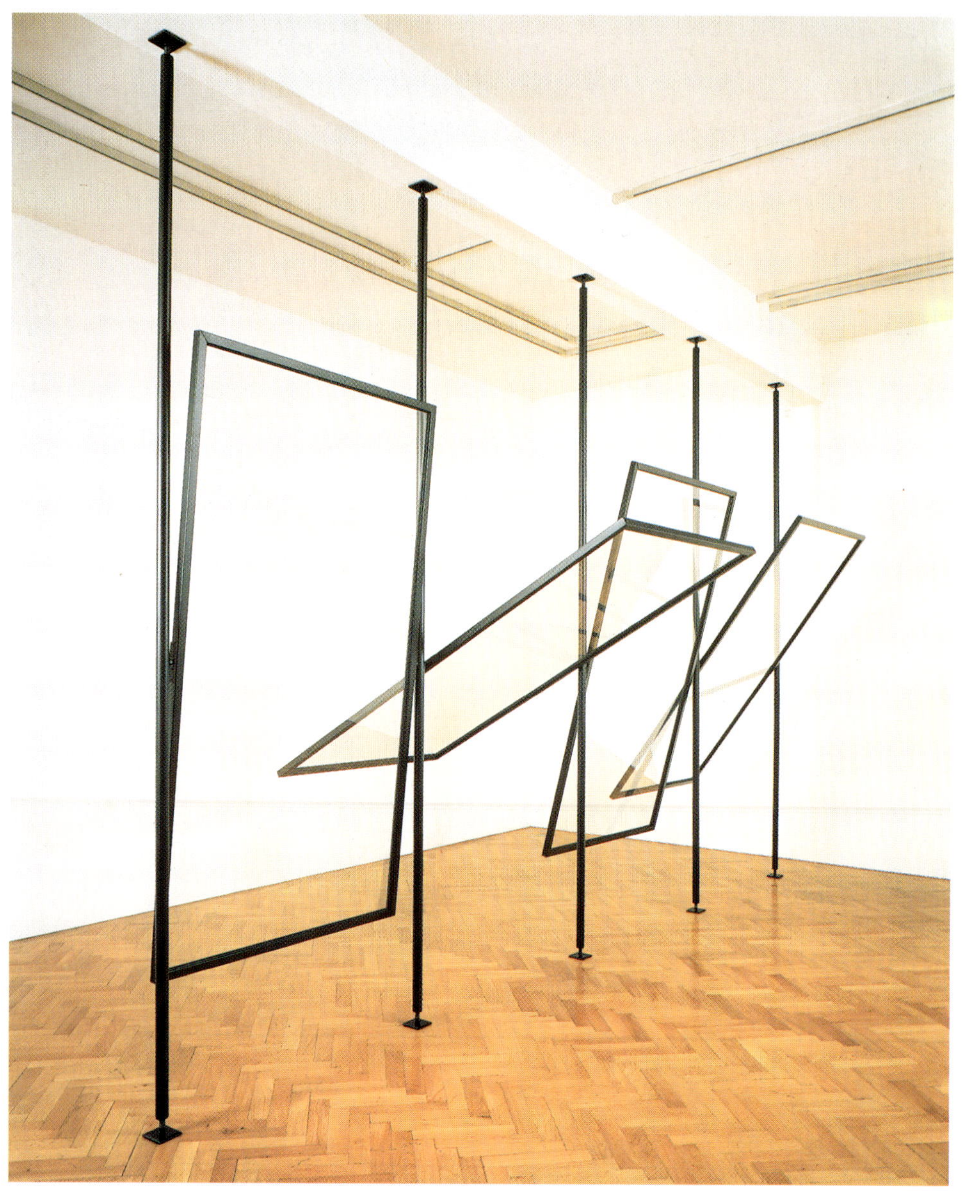

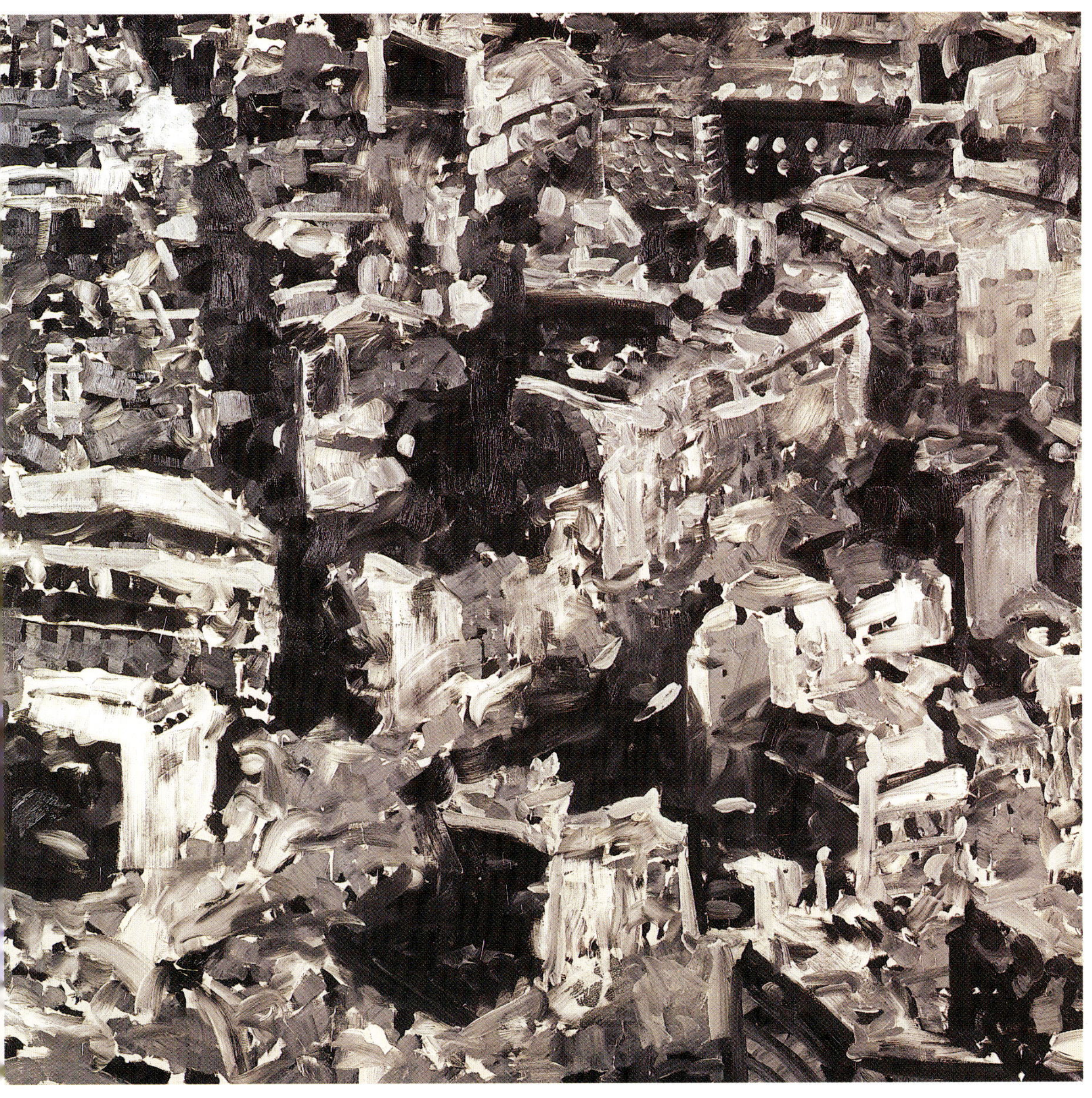

5 ▶

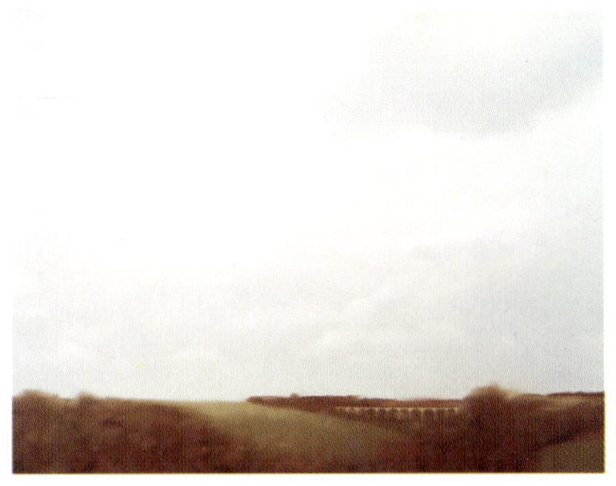

6 ▶

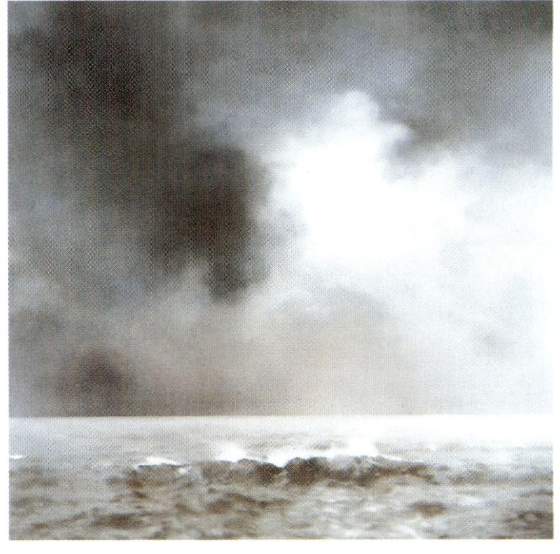

7 ▶

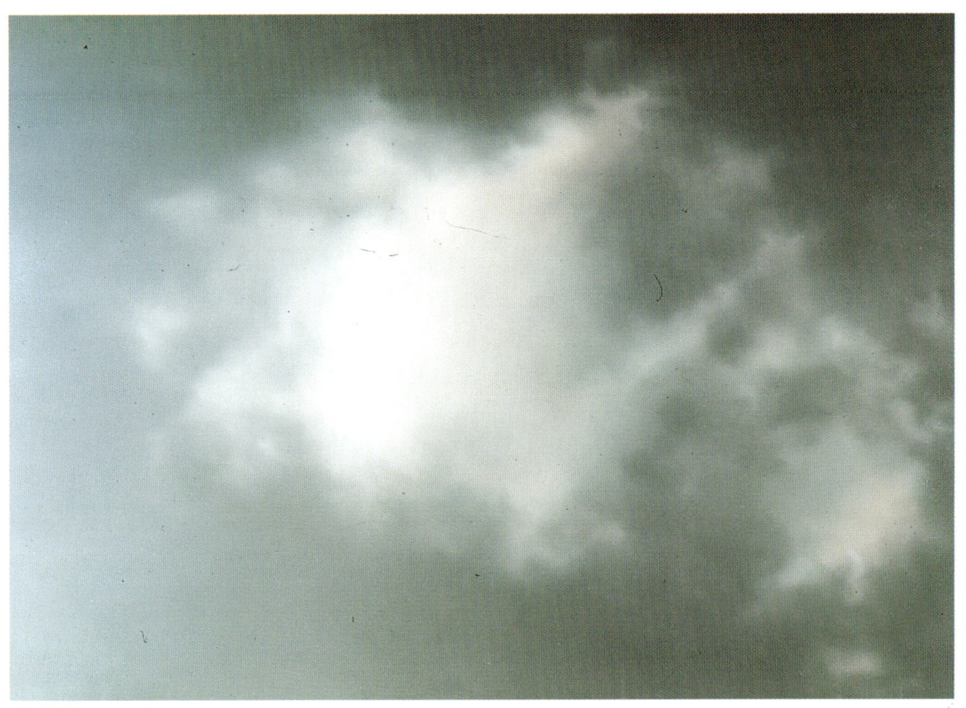

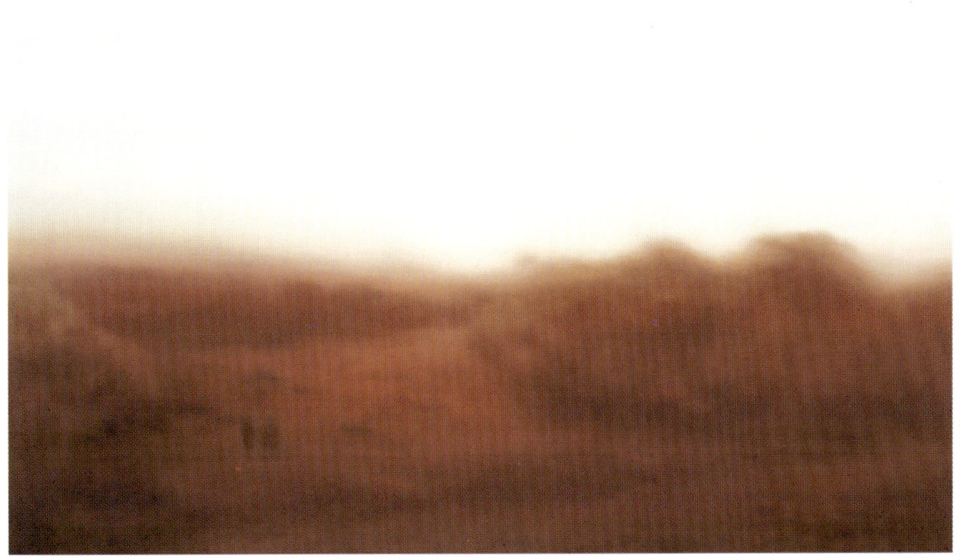

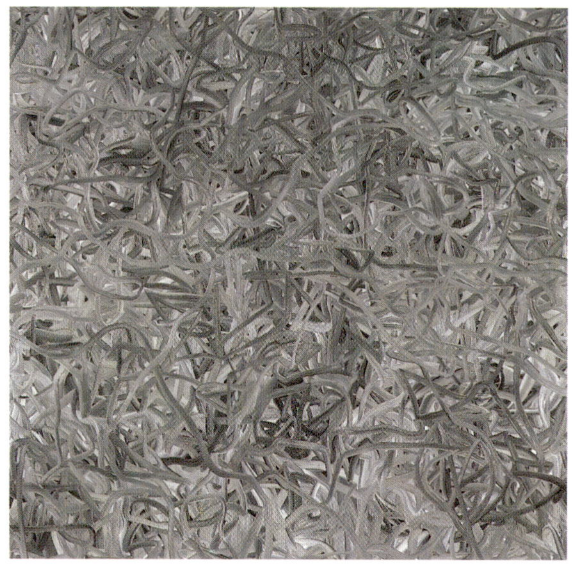

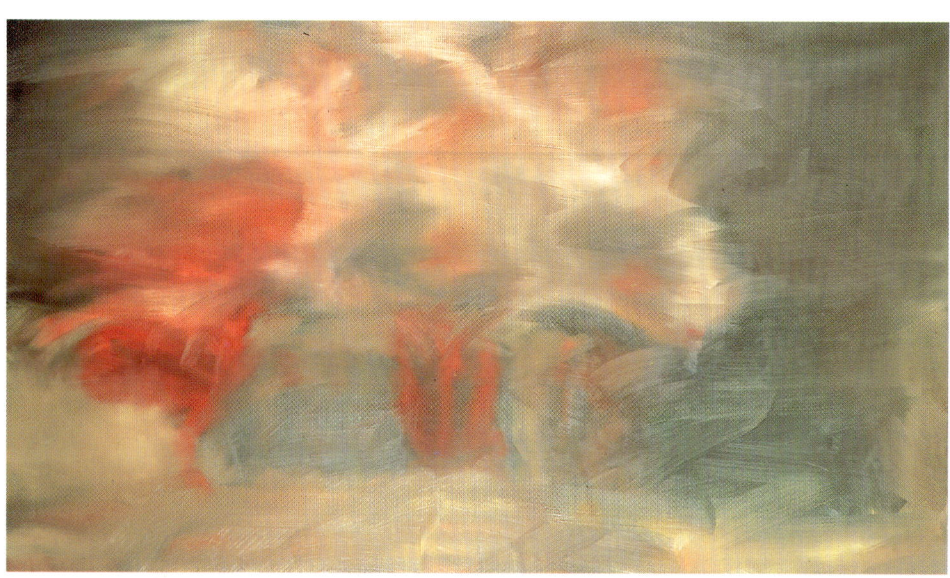

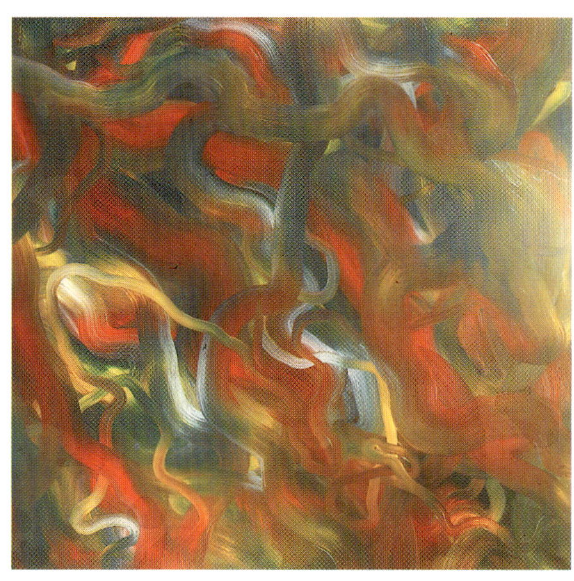

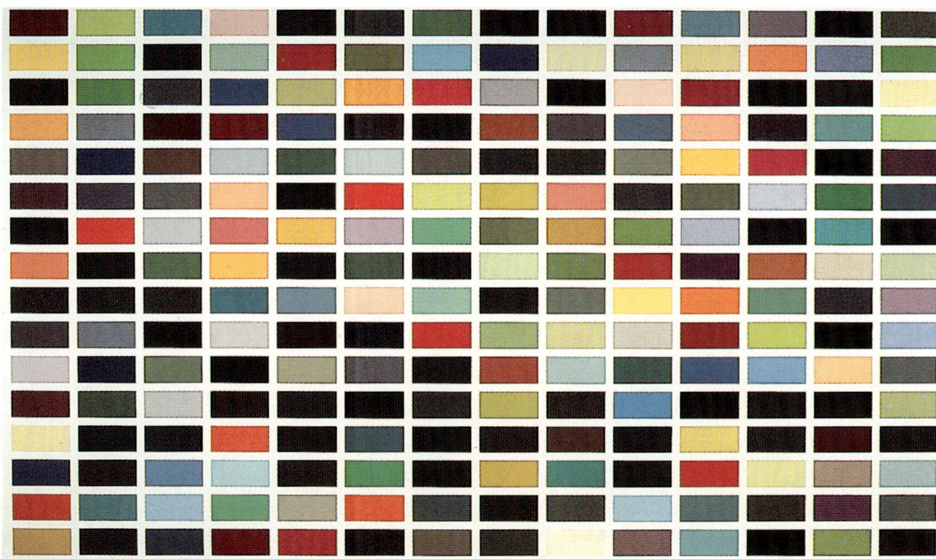

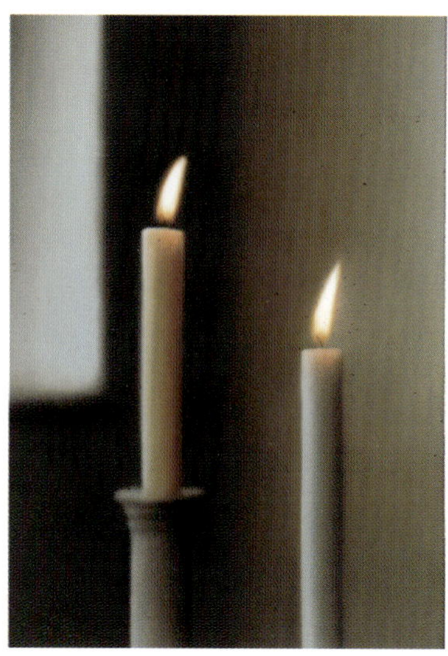

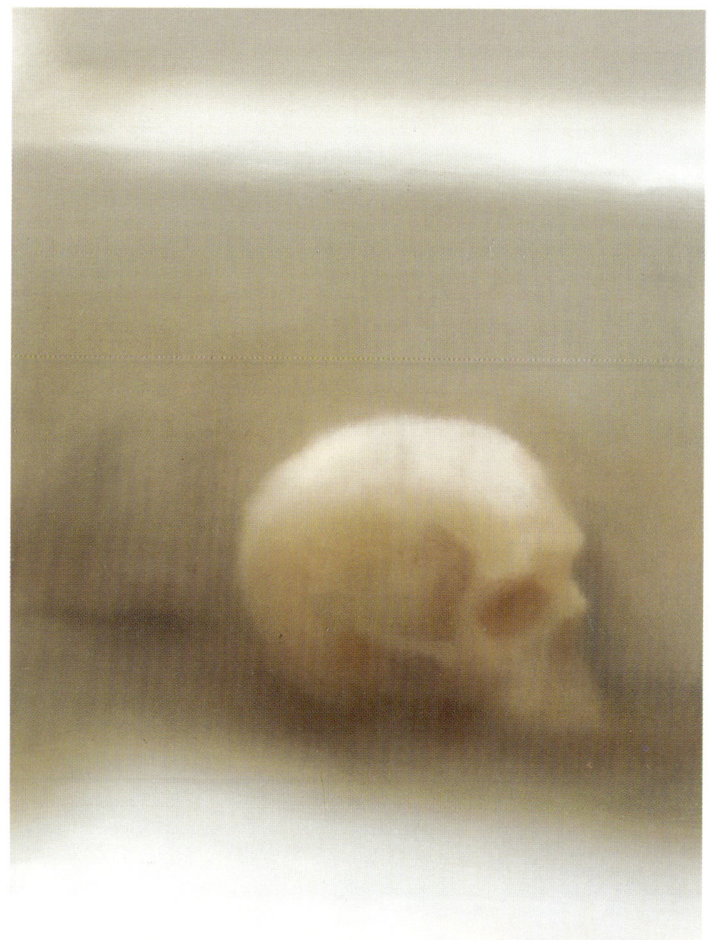

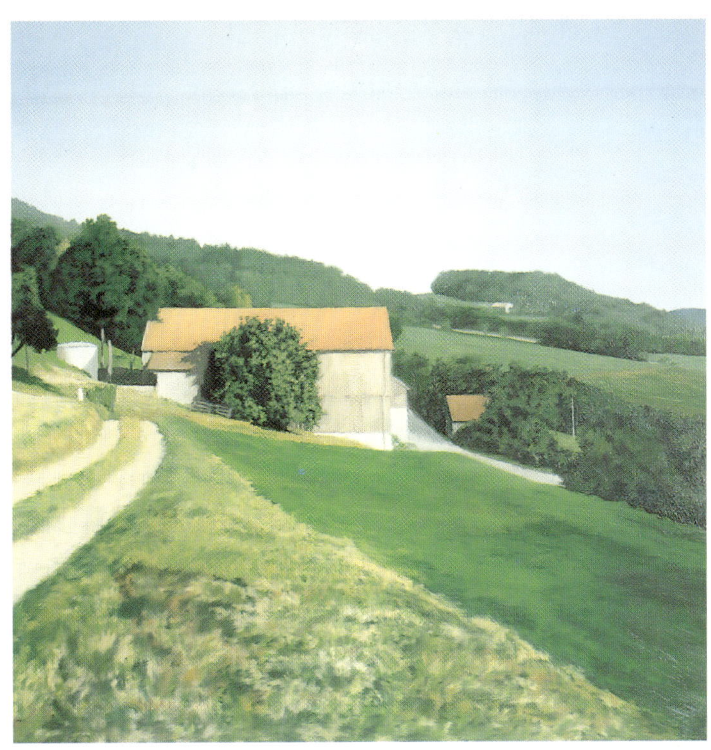

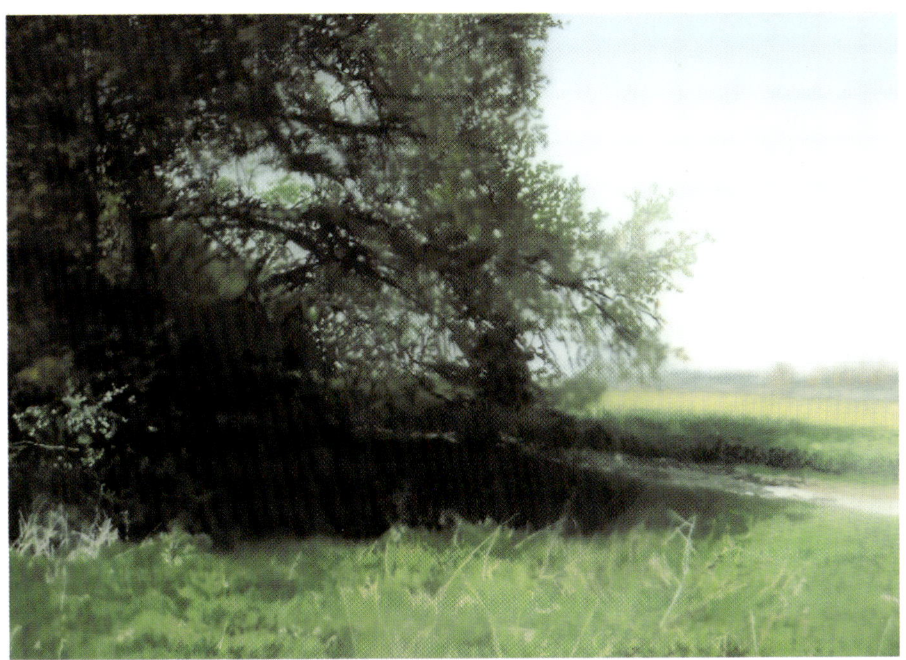

18 ▶

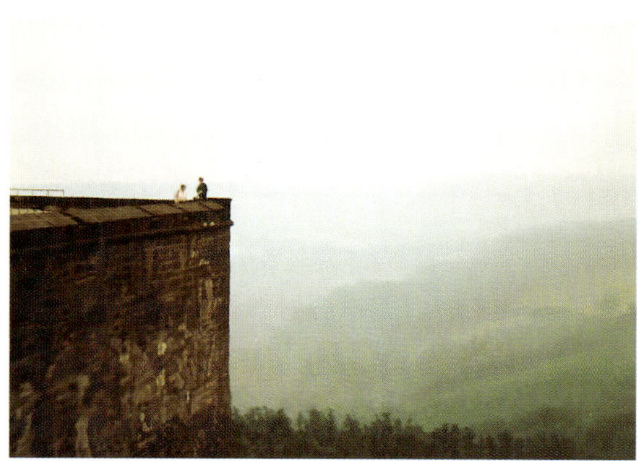

19/a,b,c ▼

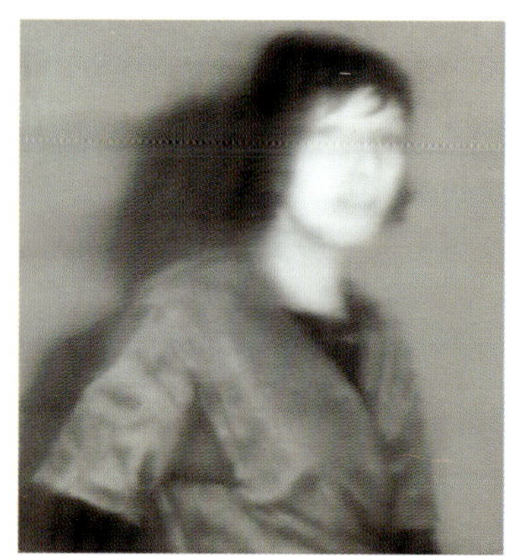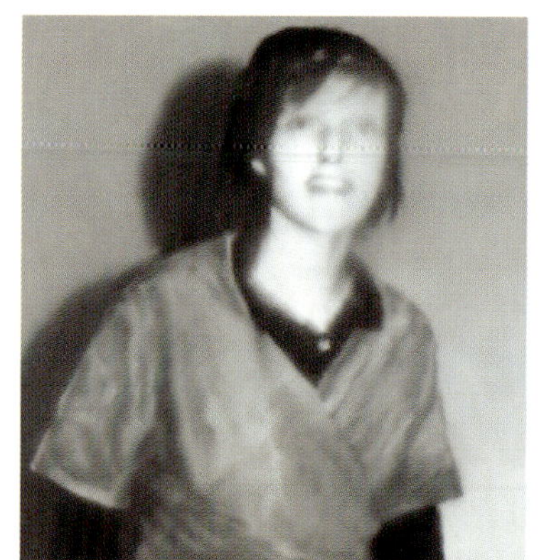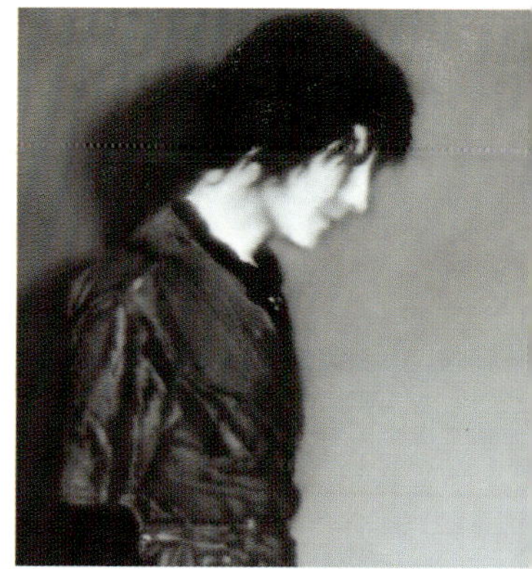

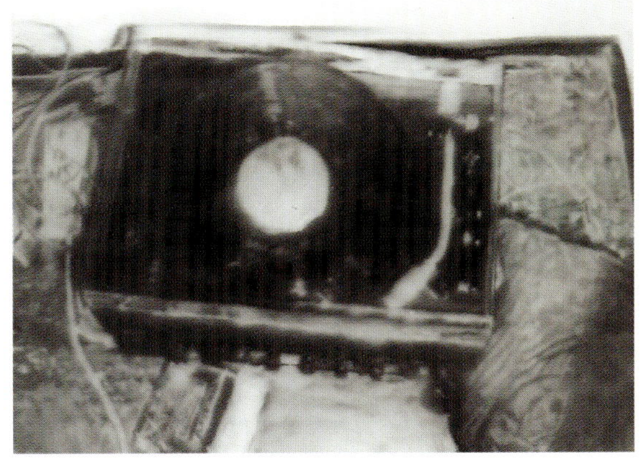

20

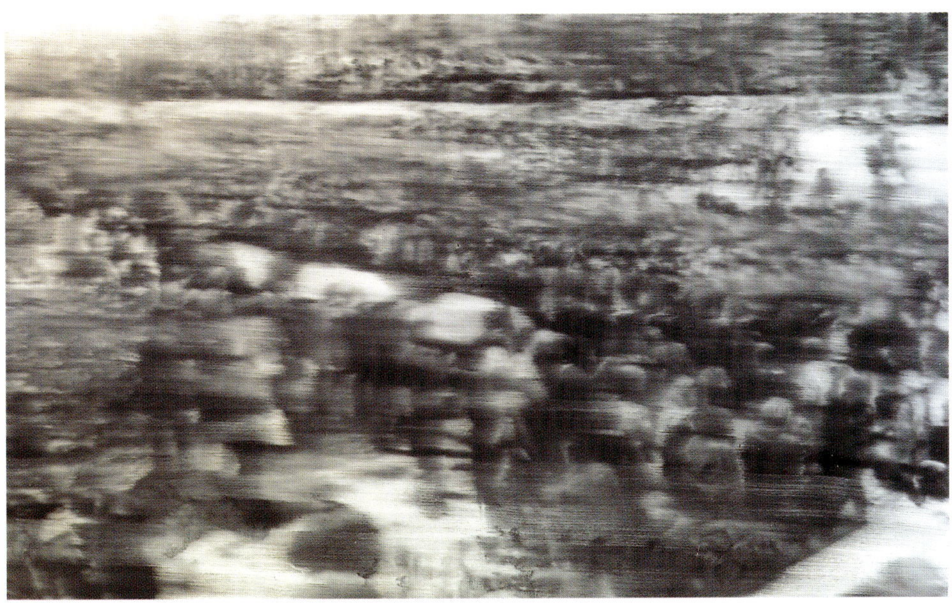

21

22 ▶

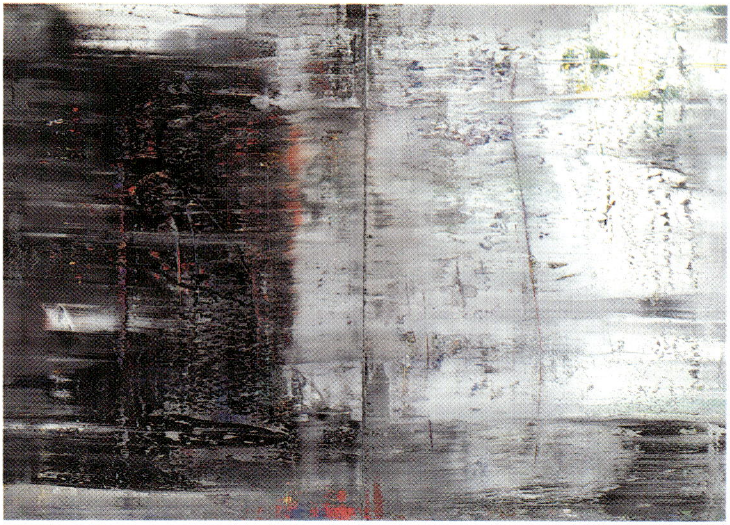

23 ▶

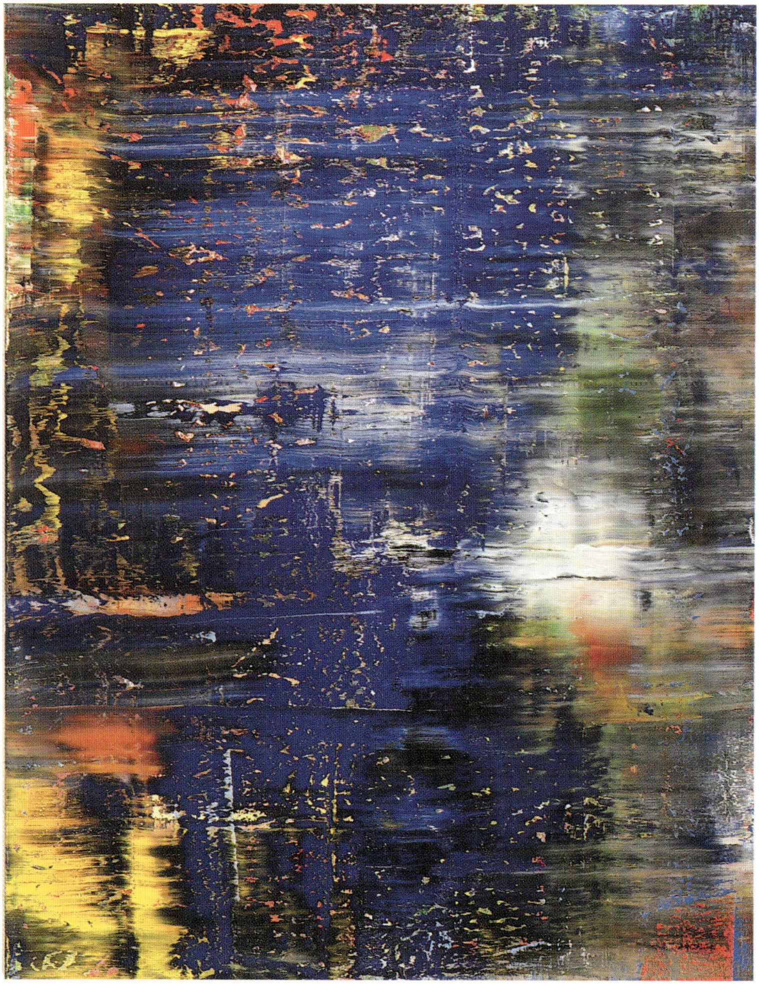

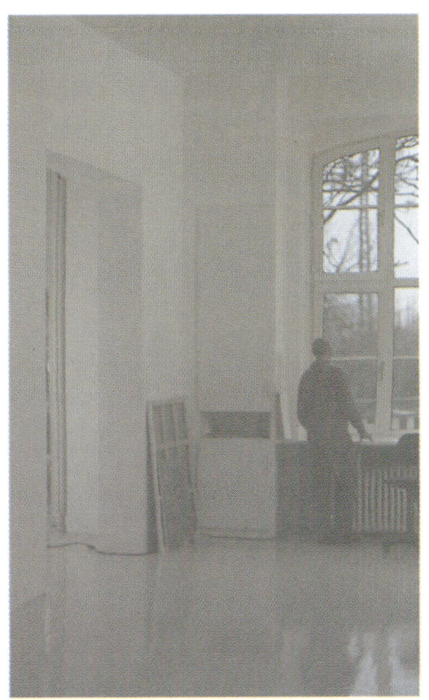

◀ 24

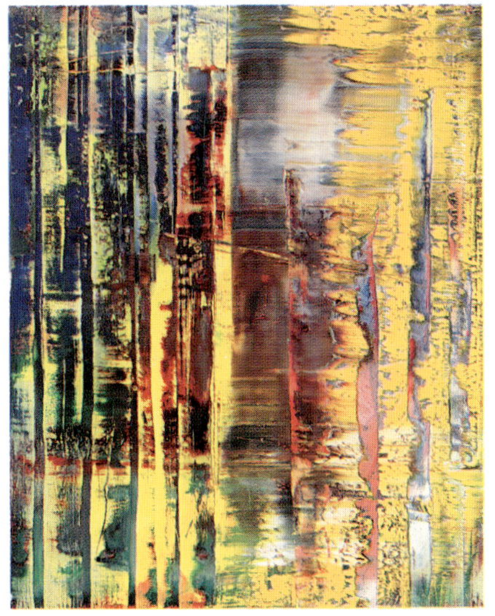

◀ 25

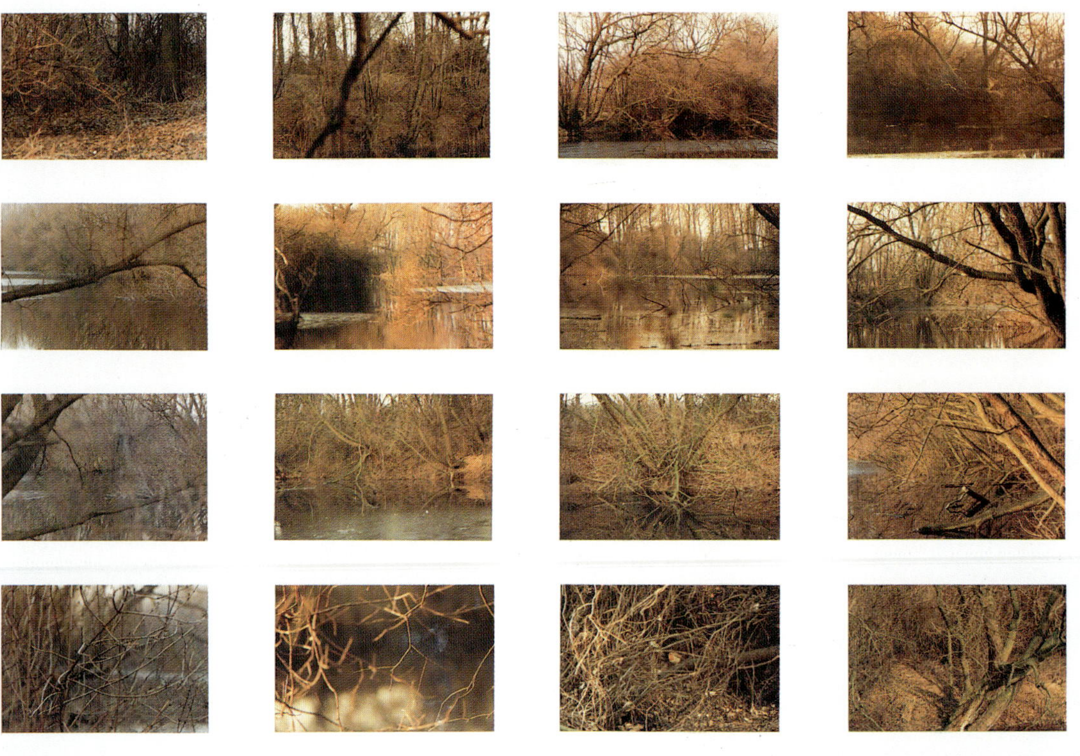

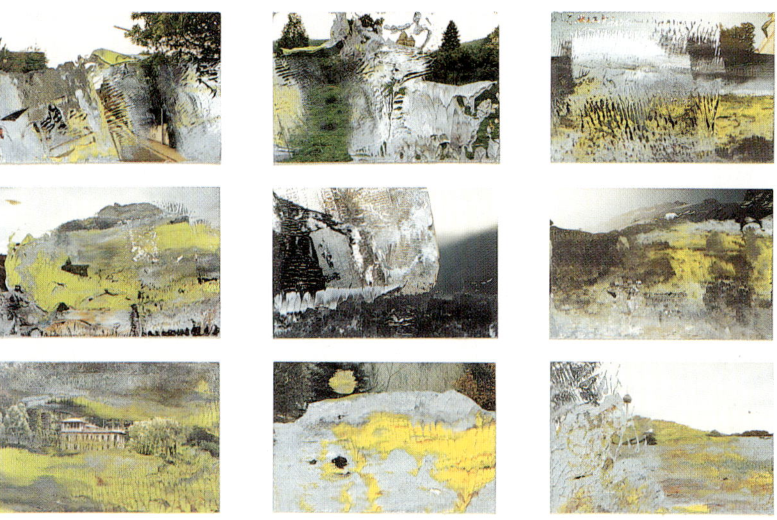

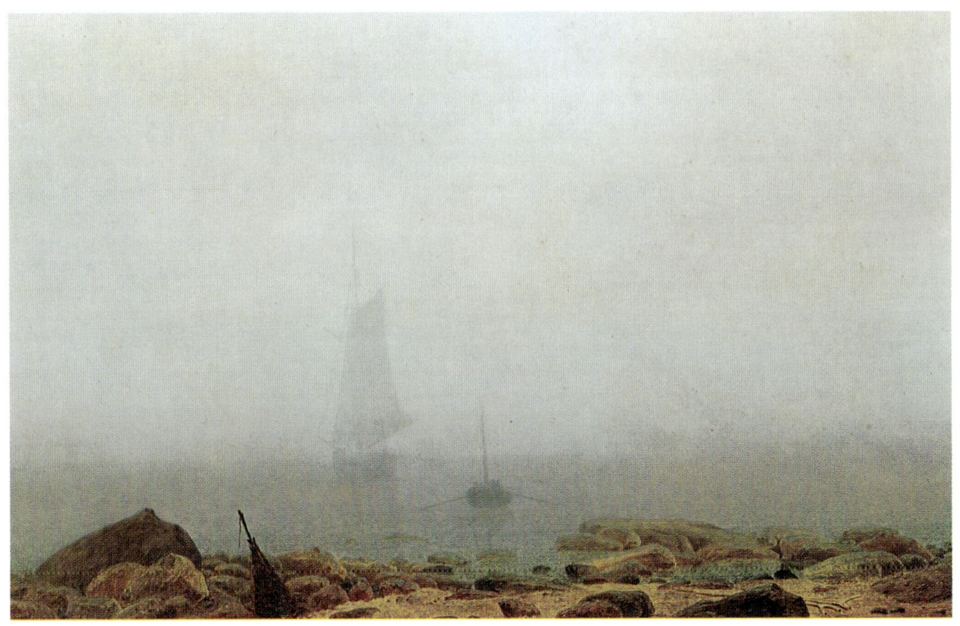

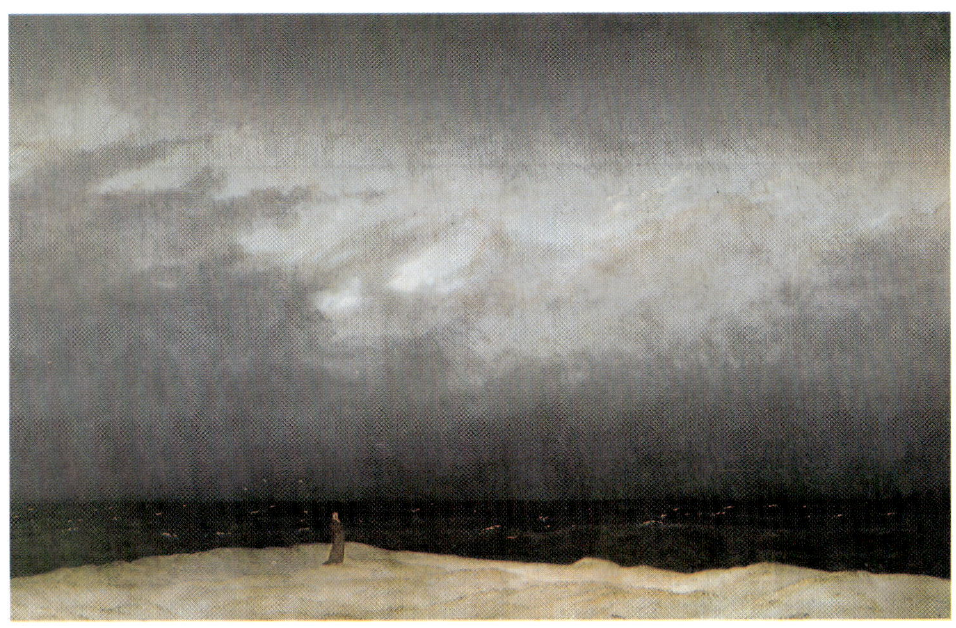

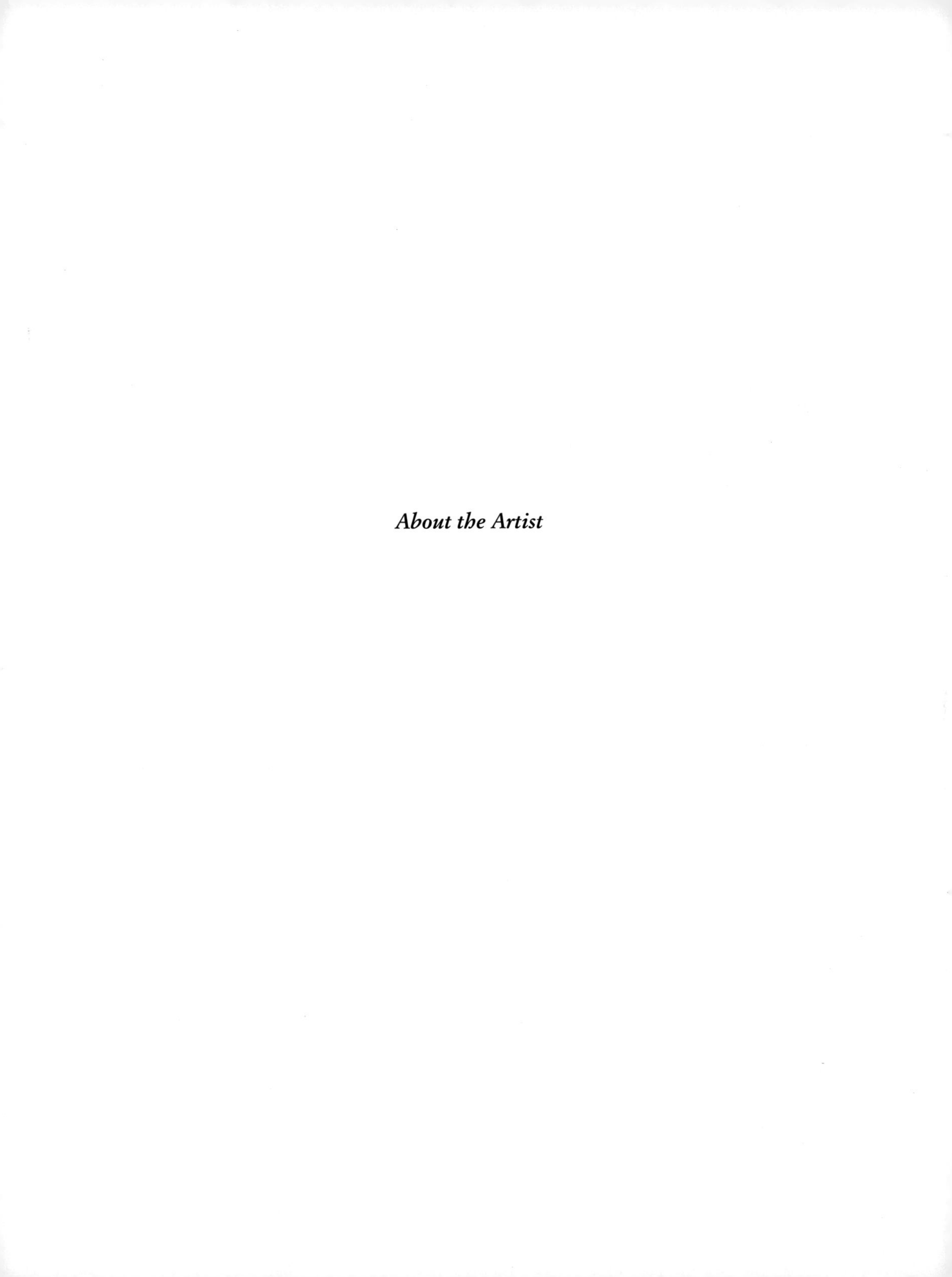

About the Artist

1932

Born in Dresden.

1948

High school diploma. Training as advertising and decorating painter in Zittau (until 1951).

1952

Studies painting (and later mural painting) at the Dresden Fine Art Academy.

1957

Obtains Master's Degree enabling him to have a studio at the Academy for three years. Marrics Marianne (*Ema*) Eufinger.

1961

Moves to Dusseldorf where he studies for two years with K.O. Götz at the Academy of Fine Arts. Meets Sigmar Polke and Blinky Palermo.

1962

Begins to reproduce photographs in oil; *Tisch,* an oil painting of a press photograph, is to be the first in a catalogue of works continuing to this day.

1964

First personal exhibition in the galleries of Heiner Friedrich in Munich and Alfred Schmela in Düsseldorf.

1966

Birth of his daughter Betty.

1971

Becomes professor at the Düsseldorf Academy of Fine Arts, where he is still teaching.

1981

Arnold Bode Prize, Kassel.

1982

Marries the sculptress Isa Genzken.

1985

Oskar Kokoschka Prize, Vienna.

Lives in Cologne since 1983.

Recent Exhibitions

1991

Mirrors, Anthony d'Offay, London.

Galerie Fred Jahn, Munich/Stuttgart.

Galerie Durand-Dessert, Paris.

The Tate Gallery, London.

Arbeiten auf Papier, Galerie Bernd Lutze, Friedrichschafen.

1992

Sils, Nietzsche-Haus, Sils Maria/Engandin.

Anthony d'Offay Gallery, London.

Frühe Druckgrafik, Galerie Bernd Slutzky, Frankfurt am Main.

Montagne Zerynthia, Associazone per l'Arte Contemporanea.

1993

Ausschnitt', *20 Bilder von 1965-1991*, Neuer Berliner Kunstverein, Berlin.

Wako Works of Art, Tokyo.

Peinture, Musée d'Art Moderne de la Ville de Paris.

Editionen 1965-1993, Kunstverein/Kunthalle Bremen.

Bilder 1962-1993, Kunst-und Ausstellunghalle der Bundesrepublik Deutschland, Bonn.

Bilder 1992 und Arbeiten auf Papier, Galerie Fred Jahn, Munich.

1994

Grafik und Auflagenbilder, Galerie Bernd Lutze, Friedrichshafen.
Bilder 1962-1993, Moderna Museet Stockholm.
Gerhard Richter und die Romantik, Kustverein Essen.
Bilder 1962-1993, Centro Reina Sofia, Madrid.

Selected Bibliography

Buchloh, Benjamin, H. D., "The Allegories of Painting and Pandora's Painting: from Abstract Fallacies to Heroic Travesties", in *Gerhard Richter Documenta IX, 1992*; Marian Goodman Gallery, 1993; Marian Goodman Gallery, New York, 1993.

Butin, Hubertus, "Gerhard Richter, Editionen 1965-1993", Kunsthalle Bremen, 1993.

Criqui, Jean-Pierre, "Drei Impromptus über die Kunst Gerhard Richters," in *Parkett* #35, 1993.

Gidal, Peter, "Endlose Endlichkeit," in *Parkett* #35, 1993.

Haase, Amine, "Wie ein Schreiner," in *Kölner Stadt-Anzeiger,* December 11, 1993 (interview).

Hickey Dave, "Richter in Tahiti," in *Parkett* #35, 1993.

Lepik, Andres, "Hundert Meisterwerke," in *Neue Zürcher Zeitung,* December 18, 1993.

Metken, Günter, "Triumph der Malerei," in *Süddentsche Zeitung,* October 25, 1993.

Nowald Karlheinz, "Zu Gerhard Richters Bildern", in catalogue *Gerhard Richter 'Ausschnitt' 20 Bilder von 1965-1991*, Neuer Berliner Kunstverein, Berlin 1993.

Obrist, Hans-Ulrich/ Richter, Gerhard "Reflections of a painter," in *Frieze*, November/December 1993 (interview).

Richter, Gerhard, *Text, Gesammelte Schriften und Interviews*, Hans-Ulrich Obrist (ed.), Frankfurt am Main, 1993.

Richter, Gerhard/ Debailleux, Henri-François "Montrer ce que je veux ," in *Libération*, October 5, 1993 (interview).

Romain Lothar, "Gerhard Richter. Arbeiten auf Papier ," in catalogue *Gerhard Richter. Arbeiten auf Paper*, Städtische Galerie Quakenbrück, 1993.

Spies, Werner, "Emotional und eisig," in *Frankfurter Allgemeine Zeitung*, October 20, 1993.

Glozer Laszlo, "Beständige Bildstörung," in *Süddeutsche Zeitung*, January 17, 1994.

Schmitz Rudolf/Richter, Gerhard in *FAZ Magazin*, January 7, 1994.

Butin, Hubertus/Friese Peter, "Gerhard Richter - ein deutscher Romantiker ?" and "Von der Kunst des Zuspätkommens" in *Katalog zur Ausstellung*, "Gerhard Richter und die Romantik" in *Kunstverein Ruhr*, Essen.

Weber, John S., " Public Information - Gerhard Richter," in *Katalog zur Ausstellung Desire*, Desaster, Document, SFMOMA.

Spies, Werner, «Laudatio auf Gerhard Richter», in *Jahreshefte der Kunstakademie Düsseldorf*, February 1994.

Butin, Hubertus, "Die unromantische Romantik Gerhard Richters," in *Ernste Spiele - Der Geist der Romantik in der deutschen Kunst 1790-1990*, 1995.

Also available from Dis Voir

Manoel de Oliveira
Les Cannibales

CINEMA

Paul Virilio, Carole Desbarats, Jacinto Lageira, Danièle Rivière
Atom Egoyan

Michael Nyman, Daniel Caux, Michel Field, Florence de Mèredieu,
Philippe Pilard
Peter Greenaway

Christine Buci-Glucksmann, Fabrice Revault d'Allonnes
Raúl Ruiz

Yann Lardeau, Jacques Parsi, Philippe Tancelin
Manoel de Oliveira

CHOREOGRAPHY

Paul Virilio, René Thom, Laurence Louppe, Jean-Noël Laurenti, Valérie
Preston-Dunlop
Traces of Dance - Drawings and Notations of Choreographers

ÉDITIONS DIS VOIR : 3, RUE BEAUTREILLIS - F-75004 PARIS
PHONE (33 - 1) 48 87 07 09 - FAX (33 - 1) 48 87 07 14

ACHEVÉ D'IMPRIMER
EN JUILLET 1995
SUR LES PRESSES
DE
L'IMPRIMERIE F. PAILLART
À ABBEVILLE

DÉPÔT LÉGAL : 3ᵉ TRIMESTRE 1995
Nᵒ. IMP. 9353